THE GREATER REALITY

AN ATTITUDE OF GRATITUDE— LIVING VICTORIOUSLY

Glenn W. Loy

Copyright © 2014 by Glenn W. Loy

The Greater Reality
An attitude of Gratitude – Living Victoriously
by Glenn W. Loy

Printed in the United States of America

ISBN 9781498410458

All rights reserved solely by the author. The author guarantees all contents are original and do not infringe upon the legal rights of any other person or work. No part of this book may be reproduced in any form without the permission of the author. The views expressed in this book are not necessarily those of the publisher.

Scripture quotations taken from the Holy Bible, New International Version (NIV). Copyright © 1973, 1978, 1984, 2011 by Biblica, Inc.™. Used by permission. All rights reserved.

www.xulonpress.com

CONTENTS

Introduction v

Lulu 11
Leroy 13
Tammy 15
Randy 19
Dennis 22
Vindla 24
Naomi 28
Harold 31
Clyde and Becky 33
Byron 36
Sean 59
Carol 71
Finding The Greater Reality 77
The Nature of God 82
Living in An Attitude of Gratitude 106

Postlude 116

INTRODUCTION

I grew up in a Methodist Parsonage, the son of a very dedicated, evangelical, conservative minister who was best described as "a man who tried very hard to please God." My father believed that a father and husband was duty bound by God to make sure that his children did not get misled, or go astray, while they were still living in his home. Of great importance to him was that we did not get tainted by exposure to Hollywood. Because television was not in our part of the world yet, I did not get to see anything even resembling a movie until 1951. That is when Hollywood produced the award winning movie *Quo Vadis*. For some reason, Dad was convinced that it would be good for me to see that one. *Quo Vadis* is a Latin phrase which translates, "Whither goest thou?" Today, and in our language, we would say, "Where are you going?"

It was an epic film made by MGM[Comp: underlined text are links. Please set as such in ebook] in Technicolor. It was directed by Mervyn LeRoy, produced by Sam Zimbalist, from a screenplay by John Lee Mahin, S. N. Behrman, and Sonya Levien. They adopted the play from Henryk Sienkiewicz's classic 1896 novel *Quo Vadis*.

The title refers to an incident in the life of the apostle Simon Peter. Peter is fleeing from likely crucifixion in Rome at

The Greater Reality

the hands of the government, and along the road outside the city he meets the risen Christ.

Peter asks Jesus, "Quo vadis?" (Whither goest thou, Lord?)

To which He replies, "Romam vado iterum crucifigi." (I am going to Rome to be crucified again.)

In that encounter, Peter regains the courage to continue his ministry. He returns to the city where he will eventually be martyred by being crucified upside-down.

This conversation is in reality, based on the conversation recorded in the Vulgate translation of the Bible, at John 13:36, where Peter asks Jesus the same question. To which Jesus responds, "Whither I go, thou canst not follow me now; but thou shalt follow me."

As the movie *Quo Vadis* begins, soldiers are marching four abreast on the Apian Way, to the sound of many drums beating out a deep and powerful military marching cadence.

Against that background, a deep-voiced narrator says:

"This is the Apian Way, the most famous road that leads to Rome as all roads lead to Rome. On this road march the conquering legions. Imperial Rome is the center of the empire and undisputed master of the world."

"But with this power inevitably comes corruption. No man is sure of his rights. The individual is at the mercy of the state. Murder replaces justice. Rulers of conquered nations surrender their helpless subjects to bondage. High and low alike become Roman slaves, Roman hostages. There is no escape from the whip and the sword."

"That any force on earth can shake the foundations of this pyramid of power and corruption, of human misery and slavery is inconceivable."

"But thirty years before this day a miracle occurred. On a Roman cross in Judea a man died to make men free. He spread the gospel of love and redemption. Soon that humble cross is destined to replace the proud eagles that now top the victorious Roman standards."

Introduction

"This is the story of that immortal conflict."
Four more movies with very similar themes were produced in 1953 and 1954.

After *Quo Vadis* I was privileged to watch *The Robe*, *Demetrius and the Gladiators*, and *The Silver Chalice*. It was my privilege to see each of them several times. As I watched these first four films in my young life, they of course, made a great impact on me. The films were well researched, and the depictions of Christians dying in the arena during that first century lay heavy on my mind. In the weeks and months that followed, I found myself reliving those scenes. Then and now, I find myself wondering if people true to the faith might not experience those times again.

There were significant moments and scenes from these movies that really stuck in my young mind. From *Quo Vadis*, there were several times that Nero would point out that people who were not afraid to die were not normal. He could not understand how people facing both pain and death could die smiling, singing, and without fear. Nero focused on that fact because it was the suffering and pain of others dealt out by his inner sickness that gave him pleasure and satisfaction. He paced back and forth, driving himself crazy because he could not fill the Christians with fear. They died singing hymns. They were supposed to bring him joy by dying with screams. A seer tried to explain to a Roman official that the Christians faced these times of trial in that victorious way because they were under a spell. From *The Robe*, the emperor Caligula examined the corpses in the arena after their execution. He also pointed out that dying without fear was not normal.

As I studied this, I could not help but ask myself if that day came, would I be able to stand without fear? Could I face death in a positive and victorious way? One thing I was very sure about. If you could face death, either by yourself or with loved ones, positive and singing while you died, there was something very real that sustained you. And, I knew it was something far deeper than the explanation of a "spell."

In a funeral manual which I have used extensively over the years, there is a paragraph that speaks to this subject. "In the early days of the church, Christians were persecuted and thrown into the arena to be devoured by hungry lions. Nero, the conceited emperor, watched from the Coliseum. As the Christians knelt in prayer, looking heavenward, a strange light showed on their faces. The hilarious Nero cried out, 'What are they looking at? What do they see?' Someone nearby answered, 'They see the resurrection of Jesus'" (Funeral Services, by James L Christensen, Fleming L Revell Co., p.58). In these situations and conditions of human misery, there is something more than the experiencing of an illusion or delusion connected with some sort of imaginary vision.

Over the years, I have come to realize a great truth. These people were caught in a reality that one could not miss. It was very visible to those watching. But, there was a greater and unseen reality that carried them over the reality that the human eye could see. Think about that phrase . . . a greater reality, which we could not see, carrying them over, beyond, or through that present reality which we could see. Or, let's word it even better, a present reality which we could not ignore. Through my years of ordained ministry and a lifetime of serving the church, I have witnessed people who lived out that experience. I have witnessed people who were caught in a reality that you could not miss. But there was obviously a greater reality carrying them over the reality we were witnessing. The following chapters are the stories of some of those people I met along the way. People who accepted, understood, and lived in victory because they trusted Scriptures of promise.

As he was leaving them, Moses shared with the Israelites, "The eternal God is your refuge, and underneath are the everlasting arms" (Deuteronomy 33:27 NIV). Paul shared that

Introduction

"God has said, 'Never will I leave you; never will I forsake you.' So we say with confidence, 'The Lord is my helper; I will not be afraid. What can man do to me'" (Hebrews 13:5b-6 NIV)? Again Paul shared, "I can do everything through him who gives me strength" (Philippians 4:13 NIV). Some of these stories are dramatic, mind-gripping stories at such a level that they should be the basis for a book or a movie.

But along with those, there are countless other situations where I have observed people living their day-to-day lives in an attitude of gratitude while others experiencing the same circumstances are totally destroyed by their particular outlook on life. As you read these stories allow yourself to dwell on the following question: Why do some people control their circumstances while others allow their circumstances to control them?

There are people who everyday live in victory while others in the same circumstances live in defeat. I would suggest that living in victory or living in defeat is one's personal choice. It all has to do with your answer to the question Pilate asked the multitude at the trial of Jesus: "What shall I do, then, with Jesus who is called the Messiah?" Pilate asked. They all answered, "Crucify him!" (Matthew 27:22 (NIV)

What do you say in answer to that question? You will and you are answering it, one way or the other!

LULU

I met Lulu in my very first appointment in 1960.

That first pastoral assignment was a very closely knit small, rural community made up basically of farmers and their families. The bulk of the community's labor force worked, at least part time, in a chemical plant in a larger town fourteen miles away.

In the first few days after we had moved in, I was informed that directly across the Street from where we lived was Lulu's home. While she and her family belonged to the other church in the community, it was still expected that I would call on her. All faithful Christians in the community were expected to do this. Lulu was small of stature and at that point in her life very frail. She had cancer and was dying. But, in those last days she lived in victory. Her husband worked in the chemical plant and had a small acreage on which they lived. Her children were now grown and living away from home.

When I made my first visit, she was lying on a hospital bed in her living room. A friend was sitting with her that day. I found her to be a person of great faith. She had a very close relationship with the Lord. She loved to talk about her family, her church, and her faith. Most of the times that I called on her, she was drugged heavily to help fight the pain. Sometimes she was so drugged that she could not speak coherently. As we were visiting, a spasm of pain would run

The Greater Reality

through her. Her veins would stand out on her forehead, and she would quiver and shake. When the spasm of pain passed, she would look out the window, sometimes at a typical dark, overcast, wintry Michigan day and say, "Isn't this a beautiful day the Lord has given us?" Her conversation was always filled with thoughts of gratitude and how good God had been to her. My visits with her were intended to give her a spiritual lift. But, I always felt it was she who had lifted me. Others related the same feelings. She was a light to me and every person in that community who was privileged to know her. Lulu was very definitely caught in a reality that one could not miss. But there was a greater reality we could not see which carried her over that one we could visually see. She knew the truth of God's Word: "The Lord himself goes before you and will be with you; he will never leave you nor forsake you. Do not be afraid; do not be discouraged" (Deuteronomy 31:8 NIV). I carried her testimony with me throughout my ministry. Many times over the years I shared her story to encourage people caught in very difficult circumstances.

God did not fail Lulu. He did not fail those with whom I shared her story. He will not fail you. Listen to the promise made to you.

> And I will ask the Father, and he will give you another advocate to help you and be with you forever—the Spirit of truth. The world cannot accept him, because it neither sees him nor knows him. But you know him, for he lives with you and will be in you. I will not leave you as orphans; I will come to you. Before long, the world will not see me anymore, but you will see me. Because I live, you also will live. John 14:16-19 (NIV)

Once again: God did not fail Lulu. He will not fail you.

LEROY

Over the years, I watched for people caught in a reality which we could visually see, who were living in a greater reality we could not see that was carrying them over that reality we were seeing. In my second parish, I met another person living this reality. Leroy had served his country in the Second World War. He was captured in the Pacific theater and was a prisoner of war for many months. He was one of the very few who survived the famous "death march" of the Pacific. As I remember it, they said he entered the service weighing more than 180 pounds. He came home weighing right at eighty-three pounds.

Leroy was a very gentle and kind man, always smiling and always speaking softly. One time I needed to see him. His wife said he was working in a field over behind the church. I drove over to the field, stopped at the edge of it, and shut off my engine. I know I looked over that field and thought the same thing everyone else who ever looked at that field thought. Why in the world is he spending time on this field? It had a very sandy and light soil. The corn plants were sparse and looked ragged at best. The rows were laid out evenly, but the plants were not evenly spaced. It was obvious that many of the seedlings had simply not broken through the surface soil.

I sat for a moment, and then realized that the tractor was running, but it was not moving. I got out and walked across the plowed ground to where the tractor was sitting. Leroy was sitting there looking off into the distance. There were tear stains on his face. I gently spoke his name. After a few times, he turned and looked in my direction. Then he spoke, and the very first thing he said was, "I guess you are probably wondering like everyone else why I bother with this field?" I had to nod my head, agreeing that I had wondered.

He said, "During those months in the prison camp one of the things that kept me going was dreaming of being back home sitting on this tractor in this field, plowing this ground. With that picture in my mind, I prayed continually. It was one of the things that got me through it all, and I don't care if it ever produces an ear of corn. I am going to keep on working this ground as long as I am able to do so. Do you understand?"

I said that I thought I did.

You might be asking right now, how does this story fit into a book about people living in one reality while caught in another reality? Leroy was ill and suffering with many physical problems the entire time I knew him. He never recovered from the treatment in prison camp and from that death march that cost him over half his body weight. He never again regained his good health. But over the years I never met a man who lived with more genuine humility, more real joy, or sincere gratitude toward God than Leroy did. He was a constant source of inspiration to me.

As Paul said, so did Leroy,

> But he said to me, "My grace is sufficient for you, for my power is made perfect in weakness."
> Therefore I will boast all the more gladly about my weaknesses, so that Christ's power may rest on me. That is why, for Christ's sake, I delight in weaknesses, in insults, in hardships, in persecutions, in difficulties. For when I am weak, then I am strong. (2 Corinthians 12:9-10 NIV)

TAMMY

Our family refers to her as our "miracle child." Tammy Jo Loy was born May 24, 1960 at Saginaw General Hospital in Saginaw, Michigan. Her trials in life began with her birth. At the end of seven months, she entered the world prematurely weighing three pounds ten ounces and dropping immediately to two pounds and fifteen ounces. In the middle of the last century, they were not always able to get the oxygen set perfectly in hospital incubators. Because of this, Tammy entered the world with a touch of cerebral palsy. She had several leg operations during her early years to lengthen the tendons in the back of her legs. Most of her childhood, she wore leg braces to help correct that problem as well. Because of that, Tammy was never able to fully participate in the athletic activities of her siblings. Her artistic ability however was obvious, even during her childhood and formative years. She has enjoyed drawing, painting, and writing, especially poetry.

Tammy graduated from high school and entered college, first at Westmar College at LeMars, Iowa, and then graduating from Northwestern College in Orange City, Iowa, During her senior year there, Tammy experienced an automobile accident. The second Sunday of December, 1981, she and a friend were returning from attending a presentation of *The Messiah*, in Sioux Center, Iowa. Witnesses stated later that when the stream of cars came up on a slightly higher plane

The Greater Reality

than they had been driving on, they all hit black ice. A gust of wind caught Tammy's car, and she was blown sideways immediately and underneath a full-size van coming toward her. She ended up underneath that van. Her passenger was ejected through the right door, and landed several yards away in the ditch on the side of the road. They searched for several minutes around the area to see where Tammy was, and then someone said, "Hey, she is underneath the wreckage."

A professor for whom Tammy had worked the day before in the college library told me later that when they finally found her, he crawled underneath the cars enough to where he could hold her tongue and keep her from chocking to death. He said, "I looked at her, and did not know who I was giving aid to." She was that bad.

A piece of Tammy's forehead was missing, part of her upper palate, and part of her chin. Most of her upper teeth were driven into her jaw. Several teeth were missing as well. She had nine breaks in one leg, and several in the other. Both of her upper leg bones were broken in both legs on both ends. Bones came to the outside in three places on one leg. She had a crushed pelvis, which they did not find until later. The bones in both knees were crushed, as well as both ankles, her left elbow and left wrist.

They had to cut her out of the car with the "Jaws of Life." They kept her on life support until they got her to the hospital.

Her first operation to repair her face, "to make her presentable," according to the surgeon, took six and a half hours. Her mother did not recognize her when she was first able to visit her in the hospital room. She would remain in a coma for five days until Friday night and "coded twice during that week. On Friday night, she awoke for about forty five minutes and was awake just long enough to say to her parents, "I'm sorry." Then she fell asleep again. She would remain basically in that state, leaving it partially for brief periods over the next thirty days, as the swelling in the brain went down. When they got her to Sioux City, the miracles began.

There were three very good hospitals in Sioux City at that time. One was designated as the "Burn center," the second one was designated the "Heart center," and the third was designated as the "Trauma Center." The overhead doors at the hospital designated as the Trauma Center, St. Joseph's Hospital, were frozen down by the extreme weather. They were told by radio to bypass that hospital and take her directly to St. Luke's. At St. Luke's, there was a major medical conference going on. The best specialty surgeons in the area at the time were there.

The best doctors in the area for the two specialties that we needed most were there. Neither of them was normally accepting new patients at the time. And normally, they did not go on these calls anyway. For whatever the reason, when the call came over the speakers for the need, they came. The surgeon who worked on her face came to see us following that first surgery. Trying to prepare us, he said. "Before you go in to see her you need to understand, it will require three more surgeries for us to make her presentable." If you could see her now, you would not believe that they never touched her face again.

Because they had not discovered right away that her pelvis was crushed, they did not correct it during those first few days. It healed a half inch off center. Because they said she would already suffer a lot of arthritis from all of this, they decided not to break it and correct it. We would know later that this was the right decision. Because of the internal trauma that she suffered, Tammy has several times since that accident had to go in and have corrective surgeries. Most of those occasions have been times of great pain for her.

The greatest miracle since the accident is that Tammy and her loving, supportive husband Bill Moore have had three wonderful children. As Tammy's parents, we were afraid

The Greater Reality

that her broken body alone would be seriously challenged to sustain and do all that a pregnancy required. So we prayed unceasingly throughout each pregnancy that God would assist her. Our prayer was, "Please God, she has suffered enough. Help her form and bring this child into the world without a problem." We believe beyond a shadow of a doubt that it was the combination of both efforts, the body of the mother and our prayers, which produced those three wonderful children.

Tammy remains for our family a source of inspiration for all of us. Her siblings repeat that again and again. But, you ask Tammy and her response is that she is one blessed person. When she was diagnosed with breast cancer a few months ago, her first response was, "Well, let's see what God is going to do this time."

At the end of her treatments for cancer, this is exactly what she said to us. "I don't know what you all are making such a fuss about, I am one blessed person." What a blessing she is to all of us. She lives above the realities she faces, carried by a greater reality. Her faith is probably best stated in the following passage of Scripture: "That is why I am suffering as I am. Yet this is no cause for shame, because I know whom I have believed, and am convinced that he is able to guard what I have entrusted to him until that day (2 Timothy 1:12 NIV).

RANDY

Randy was thirty-seven years old, and the father of two young boys. He had been a state wrestling champion when in high school those many years earlier, and he still had the physique of a man who took good care of himself. Then they found cancer in the middle of his back. It was melanoma, the fastest growing type of cancer.

They performed surgery. It was believed that they had gotten it all.

He went through the usual treatments following the surgery. The cancer went into remission, but, then it came back again. This time, they told him there was nothing more they could do.

Some time later I was visiting him at his mother's home. He asked if I believed in the anointing of oil and the laying on of hands for illnesses. I told him that I certainly did. He asked if I would be willing to bring the elders of church over and do that for him. I replied that I would be glad to do that. So, a few days later on a Sunday afternoon, I had twelve of the leaders of our church gather at the church for a time of prayer, dedication of each other, and anointing of ourselves to go and perform this prayerful, sacred rite for Randy. There were two doctors in the group. One of them said, "You know I believe in the power of prayer. Glenn would not have asked me here if that were not true. I feel the need to share this as

The Greater Reality

we go. We are going because we feel led to go and do this. However, God's overall plan for humanity at this time in this temporary arena is that we grow old, we get sick, we die, and we leave this earth. We are not going to change that overall game plan that God has. But, we all feel that God is calling us to do this."

After a time of prayer, and the anointing of each other, we walked over to the home of Randy's mother where he was staying during this time. We had a time of prayer and we anointed Randy. I really felt that God witnessed to me during this time that the answer was "yes."

I was the last one to leave the house. As I turned to close the front door, Randy raised up on his elbow. He was so drugged for pain that his speech was thick and not very clear. He said as loud and clear as he could, "Hey preacher, whatever happens you tell them I won." He died a couple of days later.

At his funeral on Thursday of that week, the very first thing I shared with them was what Randy wanted them to know, "Whatever happened, he won."

This man knew he was facing the possibility of death. He knew he might be leaving his precious family, including two small sons, for the rest of their earthly lives. He wanted desperately to stay with them, but his last words facing death were, "I win." There was a greater reality carrying him above and beyond the reality that we left here were witnessing with our naked eyes.

There are those reading this who will say, "That proves you did not have enough faith. If you would have believed enough, you would never have accepted the word of the doctor who said that you were not going to change God's overall plan. You just did not believe enough."

To them I offer this answer. I would follow the words of my Lord before I ever listen to the voice of men. In his hour of greatest trial, Our Lord left us the example which He wanted us to follow.

> Then he said to them, "My soul is overwhelmed with sorrow to the point of death. Stay here and keep watch with me."
> Going a little farther, he fell with his face to the ground and prayed, "My Father, if it is possible, may this cup be taken from me. Yet not as I will, but as you will."
> Then he returned to his disciples and found them sleeping. "Couldn't you men keep watch with me for one hour?" he asked Peter. "Watch and pray so that you will not fall into temptation. The spirit is willing, but the flesh is weak."
> He went away a second time and prayed, "My Father, if it is not possible for this cup to be taken away unless I drink it, may your will be done." (Matthew 26:38-42 NIV)

Again, Jesus said, "My food," said Jesus, "is to do the will of him who sent me and to finish his work." (John 4:34 NIV).

God promises to answer prayer. Sometimes his answer is 'No." One of the secrets to being a Christian is that God is on the throne instead of self. That means listening for what God is saying, not trying to convince God of what I am saying. Too often there are those who do the latter.

Randy lived and died in victory. Like Randy, I want to live and die in victory.

DENNIS

Dennis will always hold a special place of memory in my heart. I got to know Dennis fairly well. Dennis was a guidance counselor for the Catholic grade school in the community where I was assigned. Many Sundays he would attend mass at his church and then attend services at our church as well. In that community we had a "Men for Missions" organization made up of more men from our church than any other. But with several other men, Dennis was a member of that group also. This group held a Wednesday morning Bible Study at a local restaurant. The group met very early in the morning in order for those attending to get to their jobs. Dennis was just about always in attendance. And, he also had to get to his job on time.

Dennis was a polio victim who always required crutches to get anywhere but he was very dependable in his work and was very seldom absent. Even though it was very difficult for him to get anywhere, he was faithful to many activities. In addition to required school functions and his church involvement, Dennis attended many athletic activities. He showed his support of the students from both schools. He did not like to depend on others, and tried to be as independent as he could be, so it was not uncommon to be driving down a street in his neighborhood in the middle of a snow storm and see his dark form lying on the sidewalk. You stopped as quickly as you could, put on the four way flashers, got out, ran over and bent down. With a laugh Dennis would say, "So God sent you to pick me up today."

His bright, buoyant, and always positive spirit was a source of encouragement and strength to all of us who were privileged to share life's pathway with him. Once again Dennis was one of those who lived above his circumstances and proved that it is not your circumstances that are of the most importance. It is what you do with your circumstances that determine your life and the quality of it.

There are so many appropriate Scriptures that apply to Dennis and his story. Dennis knew the truth of Paul's passage in Corinthians.

> But he said to me, "My grace is sufficient for you, for my power is made perfect in weakness." Therefore I will boast all the more gladly about my weaknesses, so that Christ's power may rest on me. That is why, for Christ's sake, I delight in weaknesses, in insults, in hardships, in persecutions, in difficulties. For when I am weak, then I am strong. (2 Corinthians 12:9-10 NIV)

I believe with all my heart, that part of Dennis's visible faith and witness to us was because of his faith in the following passage. "Now there is in store for me the crown of righteousness, which the Lord, the righteous Judge, will award to me on that day—and not only to me, but also to all who have longed for his appearing" (2 Timothy 4:8 NIV).

Dennis still remains a source of inspiration for me.

VINDLA

Her name was Vindla. When I first saw her, I was intrigued. I was a preacher's child and my father took our family to church wherever and whenever he was preaching. We had just moved to that parish on the northern plains and lived in the county seat where the main church of the parish was located. The second church on the parish was located twenty two miles south of town; I can still see its little congregation begin to gather for church. There were the Delaneys in their black '46 Chevy two door. There were the Larsons in their light blue Kaiser. There were the Fred Kierlebers in their '34 Ford ton and a half truck, their only vehicle. There was Delvin Wagle and his mother in their always-shiny bright maroon Packard. There were a few others, but those were the folks who were always there, and it is easy to recall them and their automobiles. The last one to arrive was Vindla.

Her car deserves a full paragraph by itself. She was driving a 1929 four door Dodge.

It had been a black car. It was now almost entirely rust colored. A section was missing out of the wooden steering wheel. There was no roof on it. Wires tied the doors together and held them shut. Most of the glass was also missing. However, the rear window and the windshield were both still there. But they were mostly gray-colored from the aged adhesive glue between the layers which made up the glass panels. An old blanket covered the front seat. The rear seat was gone. There was no radiator cap. That was a good thing because when it arrived there was always steam blowing out of it. In the rear area where the seat used to be, there was a ten gallon cream can. From that she filled the radiator with water each time she got ready to drive the car somewhere.

She arrived each Sunday literally hunched over the steering wheel. She was a fairly large woman who always had a great smile on her face. Several weeks after that first Sunday, we were privileged to visit her at her home and eat supper with her.

Many years earlier, she had left home and worked as a governess in New York. She got tired of the pace of city life and returned home to her parent's small farm. They had both died several years earlier and the land had been rented out until she returned. When Vindla returned home from the big city, she began life as a single woman sheep rancher.

A few years earlier the floor of her house had caved in. She just moved into the barn. There in what had been a feed room and was more than a little crowded now by her piano, we gathered and ate the meal with her. I never met anyone who was better at finding something positive in whatever she ended up facing.

At that little country church, she sat down at the piano and played for us in a manner that reminded us how well trained she was. After church, she sat and taught us children our Sunday School lesson for the day. Vindla lived above her circumstances no matter what they were.

When I was a child, often I wondered where Vindla got her strength from. She was, after all, a single woman running a ranch by herself. Later, as I studied Scriptures, I came to realize the answer to that question.

The Lord is my strength and my shield; my heart trusts in him, and I am helped. My heart leaps for joy and I will give thanks to him in song. Psalm 28:7 (NIV)

Nehemiah said, "Go and enjoy choice food and sweet drinks, and send some to those who have nothing prepared. This day is sacred to our Lord. Do not grieve, for the joy of the Lord is your strength." Nehemiah 8:10 (NIV)

I also found myself wondering, in my childlike way, how she could be so full of joy all the time when she lived all by herself. But I came to understand that also. I know from time spent in her home, that Vindla loved her life. She was a very contented person. But I also know she was looking forward to that day when her Lord would welcome her home and she would hear his words. "His master replied, 'Well done, good and faithful servant! You have been faithful with a few things; I will put you in charge of many things. Come and share your master's happiness'" (Matthew 25:21 NIV)!

Sometime later, I heard the following: A missionary was home on furlough. Someone took him into the city to show him what had happened in the market place since he had been gone overseas. They went to his room to get him for supper after a long day seeing the sights. His door was standing open a bit. He was kneeling by his beside in prayer and the person heard this part of his prayer. "Oh Lord, I thank you that today I did not see anything I wanted."

That was Vindla's philosophy toward life. As I stated previously, she was a very contented and happy person. She fully understood and agreed with the Apostle Paul when he said,

> I am not saying this because I am in need, for I have learned to be content whatever the circumstances. I

know what it is to be in need, and I know what it is to have plenty. I have learned the secret of being content in any and every situation, whether well fed or hungry, whether living in plenty or in want. I can do everything through him who gives me strength. Philippians 4:11b-13 (NIV)

When I think of Vindla, I am reminded of the Catholic radio program years ago where the priest ended every program with the challenge to light our candle where we were. He said, "If everyone would do this, think of what a bright world this world would be."

Vindla lit her candle, and her part of the world was truly a bright corner.

NAOMI

It was a great blessing that Naomi entered the world in a Christian home where her parents would love, provide for, and give her everything they could give her. Those parents gave everything they could all of her life to help her improve the situation. But all their effort would not be enough for her to have a full and productive life. She had muscular dystrophy.

The medical profession could not tell them anything. Muscular dystrophy had not been discovered yet. They did not know what it was until she was in her mid-teens. When they finally were able to put a name to it, they discovered that she had both types of this disease. One side of her body had the type that looked like she had good muscles, which in reality were only fatty tissue. The other side simply revealed a lack of muscular flesh. Her body was bent and twisted in form toward one side. She had trouble with her toes being pulled downward.

Through most of her childhood and all of her teens she wore leg braces to pull her toes upward. Walking was difficult her entire life. In upper grade school, she began using crutches in order to walk any distance. When it came to the various activities that other children participated in, she was only a spectator, never a participant.

I don't believe learning was easy for her, but she always got her schoolwork done and earned her high school diploma the year before she died. Her brothers and sisters had to help her go to and from school.

Before the discovery of Muscular Dystrophy, doctors had advised her father to force her to exercise in order to aid the development of muscles, but with the discovery of Muscular Dystrophy, doctors said to stop doing that. It only hastened her increasing weakness. When her father was told that, it was a source of great pain for him. He would never have forced her to exercise had he known it not only was not beneficial, but in fact, was harmful to her. I do not believe he was ever able to forgive himself for previously forcing her to do those exercises. I know he never got over the pain of having done it.

One of the responsibilities my father gave me was to make sure Naomi got home from school each day. Many were the times that I, not understanding or knowing better, was impatient with her. She never bit back at me, only tried to do whatever I was pushing her to do.

I shared the above in order to share the following: in all the years I knew her, I never remember my sister complaining in any way, never! I shared that with another sister. She probably spent more time with Naomi than any of the rest of us since she was the closest to Naomi in age. She said that she did not remember Naomi being a complainer either. She told me, "My sister lived with a faith that there were better days coming. And, she patiently awaited them. That day came in April of 1961. She was released from that diseased body."

My father died in October of 1978. My first thought was, "My father is watching his daughter run today for the first time." For all of us there is a great reunion day coming. What a glorious day that will be.

What was the greatest "life lesson" that my sister gave to me? She lived with an attitude of gratitude when, at least in the eyes of those around her, she did not have that much to be grateful for. But there was inside of her a faith which I believe surpassed the rest of her siblings during those growing up years. I know she trusted God with a clearer, simpler, and more complete faith than I had at the time. She knew the truth of Moses' promise to the children of Israel. "The eternal God is your refuge, and underneath are the everlasting arms" (Deuteronomy 33:27 NIV)

There are a couple of additional Scriptures that come to mind when I think of Naomi.

Jesus said, "I tell you the truth, unless you change and become like little children, you will never enter the kingdom of heaven. Therefore, whoever humbles himself like this child is the greatest in the kingdom of heaven" (Matthew 18:3-4 NIV).

Her faith was exactly what Jesus had in mind. A child has absolute and total trust in the parent. Naomi trusted God with all her being. The other Scripture is this: "Come to me, all you who are weary and burdened, and I will give you rest. Take my yoke upon you and learn from me, for I am gentle and humble in heart, and you will find rest for your souls. For my yoke is easy and my burden is light" (Matthew 11:28-30 NIV).

I am not even sure that she thought of her physical condition as a burden. She just simply lived with it, and she lived with it without complaint. I believe that Jesus met her at Heaven's gate and lifted her burden from her as he gave her that new body. I began this by saying that it was a blessing for her that she entered a home where she would be loved. I will end by sharing this great truth. Her family discovered, as many have found over the years when sharing homes with children who are physically challenged, the blessings really ran the other way. The love and purity brought to a home by children who are challenged far surpasses anything other family members can give them. I look forward to seeing her on that great reunion day.

HAROLD

His name was Harold. He and his wife were very close friends of my mother and father. He was a steady at both Methodist Men, and whatever church committee he was a member of. He was also my Sunday school teacher. To say that Harold loved God is an understatement.

Several years later, he and I were visiting about those years and what my father and his ministry had meant to him. He got a faraway look in his eyes, and tears glistened as he said, "I would see that gray Pontiac coming down the road and I knew I was in for a blessing." The reason for that statement was that he and my father wasted no time when they were together. They visited about God, His kingdom, and their place in it.

Harold farmed a fairly good-sized farm, and he milked a herd of dairy cows twice every day. He was always on time for church and Sunday school on Sunday mornings. Then he returned home to do the afternoon chores, including the milking of those cows. Then he would return to town for the Sunday evening services.

I should note that Harold and his family lived twenty miles southwest of town. The only time they ever missed, and I do mean the only time, was when either weather or illness kept them from being there. You could always count on them. They did not miss. This was so obvious to others in the church that they talked about it from time to time.

When they ate Sunday Dinner at our house, I always begged to go home with him for the afternoon's chores. One Sunday when my wish was granted, it was my privilege to go out to their farm that afternoon and help him with those chores. On the way out, I said, "Harold, people often ask how you are able to milk your cows morning and night, and still always make it in for church," to which he replied, "When you have too many cows to make it to church, you have too many cows." It was that simple.

I never saw Harold without a smile on his face. I never knew him when he was not giving God the glory and the gratitude for everything he was and for everything he had. Several years later, he had lost his farm due to many factors. When I visited him at his home in town, he was still the same. His motto was give God the glory, great things He has done. He was then, and now down memory lane, an inspiration to me.

The first Scripture that comes to mind when I think of Harold is this one: "Dear friends, since God so loved us, we also ought to love one another. No one has ever seen God; but if we love one another, God lives in us and his love is made complete in us" (1 John 4:12 NIV). Harold lived his faith. He shared the love of God with anyone wherever and whenever he had the opportunity to do so.

The second scripture that comes to mind is the following one: "His master replied, 'Well done, good and faithful servant! You have been faithful with a few things; I will put you in charge of many things. Come and share your master's happiness' (Matthew 25:21 NIV)! Harold was faithful to his Lord and Savior. Once he met the Savior, he never looked back. He lived in gratitude every day of his life

CLYDE AND BECKY

For several years it was the privilege of my wife and I to work close beside a very dedicated young couple. Clyde served on our church staff as the youth pastor and also assisted with the music program of the church. He had formerly been a high school wrestling coach and choir director. He and his wife were a delight to work with, and we cherish those special years.

Several years after we went our separate ways, Clyde returned to school and finished his seminary work and became a pastor. He is a very good pastor. He took a solid, but somewhat sleepy church, brought it to life, and multiplied it. It is now a fairly large and very active congregation, and I am sure the congregation would affirm this assessment. Clyde gives the credit to God and to the church members.

A few years ago, his wife was diagnosed with cancer. She, her husband, her daughters, and the church family have battled it with great courage. As I was nearing the finishing of this book, there was a new development. They hit a roadblock that seemed insurmountable. Clyde made the announcement to his congregation on Easter Sunday morning, 2014. I asked his permission to copy his letter to the congregation the following week.

This is living in victory in the face of what the world would view as defeat.

The Greater Reality

The following is his letter:

What a beautiful Easter Sunday we had! I know we have all been praying that maybe we could get one Sunday morning when all the best of this place called South Dakota could be shown to us. We got it on Sunday! I hope you were all able to enjoy the day and get out in that air. I'm sure a number of folks were gone Sunday to friends or relatives, but with that being said, you missed a good one.:) It was probably the best Sunday of attendance we have seen at Community. The 9 am service was extraordinary. People just kept coming in and coming in. The guys went for the folding chairs and set up about 150 of those... it was really something. It was so exciting to be a part of that day. It was nearly overwhelming. We are becoming a very large church family and that is a testament to your kindness and openness to friends who need a place to call home. It was an amazing day! With that said... it was also a day that I do not want to have to repeat again. The news to share about Becky was very hard. Monday, we went to talk to her doctor about what's next and she has made the decision not to do any more chemo. She is done with that. There are so many "God Things" in that decision... too many to outline in this letter... so many affirmations that came without any planning on our part.
This entire journey has been filled with so much wonder that one cannot miss the fact that God is walking close with us all. The cancer is going to do what it is going to do, we are going to do what we are going to do, and God is going to be there... we just know it! We as a family "Live in Resurrection." We don't know how long or when, and frankly we aren't concerned about that. We are not going to live these

moments wondering about any of that. We are going to live each day in the wonder of it all, and enjoy the time we have. I would hope all of you can do that with us. I have no special words that can give light to what this is like. I don't have a "sermon" that can explain what is going on in my soul, but I know that I am so not alone in this. The gift of God's presence is so evident in my day... my cup is overflowing. And if you are wondering if I ever cry or feel bad... if I ever hurt... or if I get a little frustrated with it all, the answer is; yes I do! I am not Superman!

However, I have a greater One who is real. He is greater than all this... I'm being held up by His power and grace... it is an amazing ride right now. So for all of you reading this continue to pray for healing because this is what we do. Continue to ask God for His power to be displayed as we "all" journey this road together.

There is more "kingdom" work to be done and right now is not a time of defeat, but a time for growing deep. Thanks everyone for your kind words and warm hearts... our family is so blessed by who you are. Go God Go!

BYRON

One of the greatest witnesses to the victory that one can find in Jesus Christ in spite of life's circumstances is my nephew, Byron Loy. He shares his story from the inside out. Read as he reveals one of the greatest examples of living in an attitude of gratitude in the face of physical limitation you will ever be privileged to witness.

Life is hard. Everyone has a time when their life hits the wall. How do we face the adversity? We can simply "get through it," we can become angry and resentful, or we can turn heads by doing it with a good attitude. You see, it's an opportunity. It's an opportunity to show the world that we have a great God that we serve. He is with us in the midst of the pain. Anyone can grumble and complain, but will you choose to be different and be an overcomer?

People ask me the question, "How did you get in your wheelchair?"

I could answer that "I use a transfer board" but I don't think that is what they are really asking.

Sometimes people ask, "Was it an accident?"

I'm tempted to joke that "No. It was on purpose." (You kind of see how my mind works.) To really answer them seriously, or at least as seriously as I am able, I would have to give you a little background to what led up to my eventful night. However, I must emphasize that I m not a philosopher or theologian. This is just my story about how I have tried to make sense of what some might believe was a senseless tragedy.

I was a senior in high school and had just come off of a great senior football season. Over the summer Coach Furno had introduced me to the head coach of Northern Michigan University where I hoped to play football after graduating from high school. This was before I had been selected to the All-Area team and as a unanimous pick for All-Conference as an outside linebacker (or defensive end). Beyond a handshake I will never know what would have come from my college football career.

I had always been active in my church youth group and sang for a group called "Satisfaction" that was part of Youth for Christ. I was vice president of my senior class at school, vice president of my youth group at church, and... well... I was overcommitted. It finally came to a head. I turned eighteen on a Sunday and had all sorts of birthday parties throughout the weekend. On the following Tuesday, I went to school and then to weightlifting. (I sometimes lifted six days a week) Of course, the whole point of weightlifting is to exhaust your muscles. When I got home I thought I would do a little homework and then go to bed. But, there was roller-skating with the church youth group. I never missed roller-skating if I could help it. The teens in our group were tight, and, they were a blast to be around. Regardless of how fun it was, I should have known I was still too tired to go.

I had never gone out with Jodi before, but she lived in Mount Morris, Michigan, where the Skateland rink was. I called her up and asked her out, and she wanted to go. We had a great time, and she liked the people from our church. I knew she would. When it was over it took a while to check in our skates. Like a typical teenager, I was hungry by the time I stopped to drop her off at her house, so she made me some Sloppy Joes before I left.

The Greater Reality

When I pulled out of her driveway in my parent's black Vet, it was about 11:15 or 11:30 at night. (It was a black, diesel, four-door Chevette by the way. They never would have let me drive a Corvette. What are you thinking?) I was tired and sweaty after a long day and needed to pull over after about ten miles. I had driven tired before, but somewhere along the drive I put my seatbelt on even though this was in '84 before the seatbelt law. Suddenly adrenaline surged through my body as my head nodded, and I realized I had dozed for a second. I had had a close call. I put my window down a little, figuring that (remember this was in Michigan) I would either stay awake or I would get hypothermia, but I certainly wouldn't fall asleep. I was wrong. My head came up as I woke to the feeling of my tires hitting the gravel on the side of the road. I tried to regain control too late, and my left arm went through the glass of the side window as the car went off the road and flipped. The car violently tore into the ground as it rolled. Dirt, safety glass, and debris flew everywhere until it finally came to a stop on all four tires.

Everything went quiet. As my head rested against my chest, the seatbelt held me upright. I spit glass out of my mouth and my arm hung limp out of the window. I was in pain everywhere and could hear the motor rumble. It would falter but never stopped running. Fearing that there might be a gas leak I tried to reach for the ignition key. When I couldn't even lift my arm up, I knew I was in big trouble. I knew enough first aid to know something serious was screwed up and that I shouldn't try to move.

I thought the roof was pushing down on my head. It might have been, but in the rolling of the car, the roof had caved in the front left corner and it had broken my neck at the Cervical 5-6 vertebrae of my neck. As I sat in the car, it wasn't as though my life flashed before my eyes, but the first thought to go through my mind was, "I wonder what my family will think when I'm not there for Thanksgiving?" I'm the youngest of the seven children in the family so we usually had a big Thanksgiving dinner. My next thought was, "I wonder what people will think at school when I'm not in class tomorrow?" Then I wondered if my friends at school even knew I was a Christian. That was immediately followed by the thought, "What is God going to think when we are face to face in a few seconds?"

I feared that God would ask, "Why should I let you into my paradise if you are too ashamed of me to tell your friends about me?" That shook me to my soul. But then I remembered one of the foundation truths of the Christian faith. If entrance into heaven is based on being a good person or being a bad person, we are all bankrupt. It is not based on what we do or don't do because all of us have missed the mark. God cannot be in the presence of sin. That is why Christ died on the cross. He will go to court with us on judgment day and our case will be thrown out of court. He took our place and paid the price for our sins as a gift. I was very aware of what I had done wrong as well as what I had left undone. I had accepted that gift a long time ago, and I am sure glad. This was not a time when I would have wanted to start sorting out what I believed about Heaven and Hell.

I prayed, "Lord, please let me into heaven because of what your Son has done for me. But if you want me to live here I'll serve you here." I had given my life to the Lord as a seven-year-old so this wasn't the first time I had prayed. A peace came over me that I would be okay. Either I would be with my family or I would be in heaven. It was a win-win. I needed that sense of peace right then. I would like to say that I have had peace the rest of my life, but no. It was only the beginning of a lot of questions that were to come over the course of time.

I couldn't turn my head, but I heard someone at the passenger window. Within about fifteen minutes the paramedics and fire department were there. They carefully put a collar around my neck. They used what are called the Jaws of Life to cut the door off because it was so smashed in that it wouldn't open. As I look back on it, it is miraculous that my arm wasn't taken off in the rolling of the car. I would learn later what a gift it was and how important the use of my arms would be.

They put a backboard behind me and got me out of the car. Pain was everywhere in my neck and shoulders. They got me onto a stretcher and carried me up a lightly snow-covered lawn into the ambulance. I talked to the paramedics throughout the trip to the hospital. "They say to keep a person talking ..." I told the medic as he worked on me and tested me "... so that the person doesn't go into shock, so I'm going to talk to you if that's all right." I could have counted every bump on Highway M-15 to the expressway to St. Joseph's Hospital in Flint, Michigan. I kept talking to him all the way to the hospital.

They cut off my leather jacket in the Emergency Department. That hurt. I loved riding my motorcycle and had a lot of fun rides in that jacket. They took a CAT scan of my neck and had to pull down on my arms to get a good view of the break. They said the muscles in my neck were too thick to get a great picture, but they could see that my vertebrae would require a neurosurgeon and surgery. They had to put my neck into traction to stop the swelling from getting worse and causing more damage. To do so, they had to put a screw into my skull on each side of my head so that they could hang a weight from the end of the bed.

Eventually I had surgery, and my parents remember the neurosurgeon telling them later that "I would be able to have kids and I might be able to feed myself with a prosthetic." That was the only prognosis he gave them. What he didn't know was that the prayer chain had already started.

"*Is this a Trick Question?*"

People will ask me, "If you could go back in time and had it to do over, would you change what happened?" At face value, a person could answer, "Is this a trick question?" I suppose you could skip to the end of the book to find out my answer, but that wouldn't fully answer the question, either. I guess you would have to keep reading for me to answer the question.

A friend of Jodi called her the day after the accident and asked her if she had heard that I had an accident on my way home. She couldn't believe it. A lot of people were impacted by my accident and cards and visitors began to pour in. Some of my friends and some of my family would spend the night in the hospital so that I wouldn't have to be alone. The night of the accident I had wondered if people knew if I was a Christian or not, and I soon got my answer. I was told by my parents that a lot of people I went to school with were asking why God would let this happen to me. I wasn't the only person hurting. I may have had more of an impact on people in those few months than I had had in all of my previous years in school. I remember visitors telling me that they thought they were coming to encourage me and realized as they were leaving that it was I who had encouraged them.

In only a couple of weeks, my muscles atrophied and no one would have guessed that I had once benched 235 pounds or squatted over 400 pounds. I was in Critical Care for a long time before they moved me to Intensive Care. I lost about thirty pounds and became a shadow of the big strong linebacker I had been. In all, I was in the hospital in Flint, Michigan, for three months before my breathing was strong enough for them to fly me by jet ambulance to Craig Hospital in Englewood, a suburb of Denver, Colorado. I was in rehabilitation there for another three months, learning how to be as independent as possible. I became physically stronger and my health improved. They had wanted me to stay in rehab another month, but I pushed so that I could get back home in time to go to prom and to graduate with my class.

While I was in rehab, I saw a movie with clips of people with spinal cord injuries doing things like water skiing, racing, and so on. I remember one guy say, "If there were ten thousand

The Greater Reality

things in life that a person could do, and if I couldn't do one thousand of them because of my disability, then I am going to focus on the other nine thousand of them. And I'm going to do as many of them as I can and do them as well as I can." Then he said, "So you know, I might as well get busy." I thought, "What a great attitude!" I've tried to adopt that philosophy of life instead of sitting around and focusing on what I've lost or what I cannot do. I learned pretty quickly that if I let my mind start listing what I couldn't do or if I thought about what my life might have been like I would get really depressed so I tried not to let myself go down that road in my thought life. I didn't know what was going to happen tomorrow much less years down the road. Jesus had said in Matthew 6, "Therefore do not worry about tomorrow for tomorrow will worry about itself. Each day has enough trouble of its own."

I had enough credits after my junior year of high school that I could have arranged my schedule to graduate early. I had been tutored while I was in rehab, so I was able to finish enough of my classes for the school to allow me to graduate. So after I got home from rehab and went to the prom and then to graduation, I had the summer to decide whether I was going to a traditional college or if I would go to a trade school to study computers. In order to give myself as many options as possible, I decided to go to college. I had always heard that it is easier to go to college directly from high school than it is to try to go back later. I took a full twelve-credit load and lived on campus. A nurse came to the campus in the mornings to help me with the three-hour routine it took for me to get up and get my legs stretched, to shower, and the other aspects of getting ready for the day. I was independent throughout the day until she came in the evening for the shorter night routine.

It was hard to go from being in a small town high school where everyone knew me, to being on a college campus where I had to introduce myself. As I pushed my manual wheelchair around the campus, I didn't just have the freshman nerves.

I also was navigating around a campus of people and trying to develop my self-image and self-esteem nine months after an accident. In high school I used to ride my motorcycle or bicycle around town. But in college, I didn't even feel safe to drive yet. I used to be a muscular 6' 2" linebacker who could throw around the football or a baseball while I talked to people. I had been 215 pounds but now I was 167 pounds. I didn't know it at the time, but my wheelchair was too small. Because of that, my legs would spasm and bounce until they came off the footrests. It made it hard to get around campus when I had to stop every few yards and pull my feet back on to the footrests, especially when winter hit.

Of course people offered to help, but I didn't want that to be the focus of the relationship. I wanted people to know me. Unfortunately, I was still trying to figure out who I was. What made the biggest difference for me was that I had always enjoyed sports, but they didn't define me. I enjoyed singing, but that wasn't what gave me my worth. Academically, I had done well in high school, but it didn't crush me when I struggled to carry those four classes my first semester and only get B's and C's. It wasn't anything that I accomplished in student government or National Honor Society or riding motorcycles or anything you could see. What saved my self-image was that I had been taught from a young age, before I had done any of those things, that I was made in God's image and that He loved me. Nothing I had accomplished and no one that I had impressed could compare to that or take my worth as a human being away. In my frustration and in my grief I had to keep reminding myself of this truth.

The grief hit me especially hard three months into college because it was the first-year anniversary of the accident. Although I had regained some use of my triceps, my condition had mostly remained the same. I was paralyzed from my chest down, my hands were paralyzed and though my touch sensation was fully intact, my pain sensation and hot and cold sensations were mostly gone from my chest down. Doctors and therapists had told us in rehab that most return of movement and sensation would occur in the first year if they were going to return at all. The finality of my condition and the loneliness at school combined with the winter season threatened to depress me, but I focused my energy on studying. Medicine that I took for muscle spasms made me drowsy, and I still was trying to get my strength built up. It made it hard to study without falling asleep. Over time, pushing my chair around campus built up my arm strength and my endurance grew. Fortunately Saginaw Valley State College was fairly flat and ideal for me to build up my strength without having to maneuver steep hills.

I also made some friends in time. Three people I knew from high school were there, but they had their own friends and had different classes. It was up to me to be assertive and reach out to people. Over the course of time I found that people respected me for how I was handling my situation. I made it a point not to make my disability the focus of my conversations. Still, a number of people came to me to talk about struggles they were going through. I wasn't the only one with questions about life. Ironically, as I talked with them, I found myself answering some of my own questions that I was struggling with. I found myself getting increasingly frustrated by how people tried to avoid their pain in all the wrong ways. I had never declared a major and had taken classes that I would need for any major. Despite my frustrations and my own grief, I felt like I had more peace and confidence through my faith than many of the people around me who had full mobility. My suite mates would politely offer me a beer or a joint and I would decline. I never had been attracted to drugs, and I knew I had enough challenges without adding a potential problem. A number of girls talked to me about broken hearts and broken relationships and still, the parties in the dorms continued to go on.

As the year drew to an end I decided to pursue being a pastor. My sophomore year I transferred to Spring Arbor College to pursue a bachelor's in psychology at a Christian school because of how much counseling pastors do. I was further from home but had become stronger, more confident, and independent. About two years after my accident I got my driver's license and a new van that I could drive, using hand controls. I found it was easier to make friends, and I started dating again. During one of my classes a professor talked about the need for Christian counselors and I decided to change my plans from being a pastor and stay with a career in counseling.

"God, Why Won't You Do Something?!"

While I was in college I had opportunities to share my story by doing some public speaking in a number of different places. In school my friends sometimes got angry with God and asked why he let tragic things happen to people. Why doesn't God do something to heal some disease, take away pain, feed the hungry, house the homeless, bring justice to the oppressed, and on and on and on? As I would share about my journey to understand pain, I found that other people were encouraged by some of the ideas that had helped me. I began to formulate my belief system as I took classes in theology, psychology, and philosophy. I have come to take the stand that God created the Garden of Eden for us. He wanted us to have a home where our needs were met and we could live in close relationship with him. We humans messed that up and have been messing it up ever since. We can't just blame our predicament of living in a world that is messed up on Grandma Eve and Grandpa Adam either, because we all have done things that create distance in our relation with God and with other people.

People asked if I had considered leaving my faith. To leave my Christian faith would be like a ten-year old running away from home to punish his parents because he doesn't like the rules at home. It's not as though I would be standing on God's oxygen hose if I decided to leave my faith and to refuse a relationship with him. It is me who needs God and not the other way around. I believe that God has more on his agenda than to make me happy or to answer my questions—which tend to question his character. God already has given me more than enough. He doesn't owe me anything, I owe him everything. Leaving my faith would have been like swimming away from the life preserver and swimming to the sharks.

When we try to figure out why God doesn't rescue people in need, we usually look to him for the answer and try to sidestep any responsibility for the problem. There are a couple passages in Leviticus that I find very interesting. God commands that when we harvest our fields, that we stop and leave some of the harvest for the poor and for the animals. He promises that there will be plenty for us in our storehouses if we do. Later, he tells us that the poor will be with us always. I see God giving us an opportunity to be part of the solution to homelessness and poverty. He also knew the hardness of our hearts and our self-centeredness that keeps us from being that solution. Imagine if we used the money we currently dedicate to movies, cigarettes, alcohol, and gambling and used it to help the poor. We could sink wells, plant trees, build houses, and so forth.

While at Spring Arbor, a scripture verse that spoke to me was James 1:2-4 which reads, "Consider it pure joy my brothers whenever you face trials of many kinds because you know that the testing of your faith develops perseverance, and perseverance must finish its work so that you may be mature and complete, not lacking anything." I also heard a quote from Booker T Washington who said, "It is not what happens to you in life that makes the difference. It is what happens in you that determines the course of your life." When reading a book called *Where Is God When It Hurts?* by Phillip Yancey I was challenged when he quoted C. S. Lewis, a British author who said that instead of asking "Why me," we should ask, "Why not me?" I responded to that because I never thought myself as more special or more deserving than anyone who was not a Christian. God loves us all. However, though he offers the gift of his love and eternity with him, he has to be both our Lord *and* savior. It's a package deal. He died for any one of us who are willing to accept the gift of salvation and the friendship with him that comes with it. It is the perfect balance that only God has between justice and mercy. He satisfied the price that had to be paid for what we had done wrong, and he also demonstrated his love and mercy by being the one to take our place and pay the cost. Only he could do it because only he had led a perfect life. Even Jesus enemies couldn't find a fault in him and had to lie about him in order to have a basis for having him crucified.

I continued to study and eventually graduated from Spring Arbor and then applied at a number of graduate schools. I was accepted at Wheaton Graduate School where I pursued a master's degree in Clinical Psychology. I had been there for one semester when I met Angie Schiermann. A mutual friend introduced us to each other at the dining commons. She had been in the work world for a while but had decided to go back to school to get a bachelor's degree in psychology. We sat and talked for a couple of hours about how we each planned to use our degree. Unfortunately, we both were trying to heal from broken-off engagements and I was trying not to be attracted to her.(trying). We continued to talk over the next few months. Sometimes we would eat together or study together until eventually I asked her out. My wounded heart mended a lot quicker when I was around her. However, she shared with me that she was still feeling very hurt by someone she had dated prior to college. In an attempt to keep from getting too serious about her I also had other friends I spent time with. One day I was with a friend in the library and as we left, I stopped to say hello to Angie. As my friend and I walked out of the library and out into the snow, Angie was shocked to realize that she was jealous to see me walking out with the other girl. We were married in the summer after I graduated with my master's degree.

I began working for an emergency program at a community mental health program while Angie finished her bachelor's degree. After her graduation, we bought a house and she took a position at Evangelical Child and Family Agency (ECFA) as a case manager. I was due to go in for some testing related to my disability and needed a reevaluation. So we took a trip back to Craig Hospital in Denver where I originally had my rehabilitation. While we were there I met with a friend who happened to be there and who had gone through rehab with me. He was there with his wife and their daughter. The young girl looked about seven years old and was well behaved but seemed very bored. When we were between appointments, we asked if she wanted to go to the recreation room with us and she smiled ear to ear. Her parents said it would be fine so we took her with us. I had been around kids a lot because my older brothers and sisters had kids, and I was an uncle starting at age five. She obviously had fun and liked Angie and me, so the next day we took her with us again. Angie said for us to go on ahead and that she would catch up with us. As this young girl and I went in to the recreation room, one of the rec therapists asked me, "Is that your daughter?" Something in my heart leaped, and I wished I could say that she was.

After this Angie and I began talking about having kids. After she had been a case manager for a year, we decided to take the classes to be foster parents. We had not even finished the courses before they were offering different children and sibling groups for Angie and I to consider. She and I were open to that but firmly wanted to start with an infant. One day she fell into bed against me sobbing. Between tears and gulping for air she said, "Sometimes I think God has played a big trick on us and isn't going to give us a baby." We were both finding it hard to be patient and tried to focus on the fact that the courses were almost over. The next day I was called out of a meeting at work for a phone call from ECFA. They had an eight-day-old baby girl who had not been named yet and was still in the hospital. They wanted to know if we could take her in as a pre-adoptive foster placement, and they had not been able to reach Angie. I was confidently able to say yes. A few hours later Angie had a name picked out, and they were placing Amanda in our arms. A few months later, they called us and asked if we could take in a four-year-old. Ashley came to live with us, and we were a family of four. We eventually adopted them both and have had the honor of watching them grow to become beautiful and wise young women.

Does God Care About Our Pain?

We often get angry when God doesn't answer our prayers the way we want him to. We even conclude that he doesn't answer prayer. The fact is, he answers all of our prayers and the question *we* are answering is whether or not we will give him control of our life and yield to his authority or not. He is Lord whether we acknowledge it or not. Some prayers are answered yes and some are answered no, and some are answered not yet. Some are even answered based on our reaction and attitude. We may not be able to handle what we are asking for. He often says no because he has something better in mind for us. If we trust him we always believe his answer is the best answer.

You might consider what would happen if God always gave us what we asked for in prayer. If Christians always got the raise we asked for and always got the promotion (whether we were equipped for it or not) what would happen? What if the guy always got the girl he thought he wanted, and the girl always got the guy she wanted? If we always got the nice house with the white picket fence and the 2.3 children,... what then? Would we be satisfied? Everyone would be jumping on the bandwagon to be a Christian because our lives would be so enviable, but it would reduce God to a sugar-daddy or a Santa Claus. Ultimately it would turn him into the servant and us into the master. We would be in love with what he gave us instead of loving God for who He is. What is your reaction toward people who love or like you only when they get their way? Do you see those people as shallow? Makes you think doesn't it?

So if God doesn't immediately give us what we want or deliver us from our troubles, is there a purpose to pain and suffering, and what is God's involvement in the healing of those who suffer? There are times when God miraculously heals. Although a heart surgery or brain surgery is amazing, I am talking about a certified and unexplainable healing. Sometimes God answers prayer and heals someone when there is no relief in sight. If God has the ability to heal us, but does not, does that mean that he is callous to our pain or does not care? The Deist position and philosophy about life is that God set the laws of nature and put the universe into existence and then checked out and is not involved in the world. The Christian belief in a God who is omnipresent would answer that God does not check out but is in all places at all times. He is our ever-present help in time of need. We, like Jonah, can try to run away. It doesn't matter where we try to run to because he will be there. He will "never leave us nor forsake us." That has been a great comfort when I have felt alone such as when I was alone in the hospital or in rehab, or when I was in school or when I am alone in bed and cannot get out of bed or get someone to help me. I have to choose to believe he is there with me.

In the book of Daniel, we hear about a time when three Hebrew slaves named Shadrach, Meshach, and Abednego were threatened by their ruling enemy king. He told them that they had to bow down to a statue or he would throw them into a furnace. He challenged them with the question, "What God can save you then?" They answered him that their God was able to save them but that even if he didn't they wouldn't bow to his idol statue. They already were living that out because God had not rescued them from slavery, but they served him anyway. That king threw them into the blazing hot surface but found that not only were they not burned up, but that there were four forms in the fire instead of three. God often does not take us out of our predicament, but he does not leave us alone in the midst of it. We may not see him but we can know He is there with us. Like those three Hebrew slaves, our reaction to the circumstances we are in will be written in the history books. Some day we will be telling our story. Or, maybe the Lord will be bragging on us. Maybe someone will be telling the Lord how our reactions to suffering inspired and encouraged them to keep fighting the good fight.

Sometimes the question is raised, "Does God have the ability to heal us?" When Moses questioned how God could feed the Hebrew people when they grumbled for meat to eat, he said, "Even if we slaughtered all of our flocks and herds, would there be enough meat for all of them (two million people)?" God asked Moses in reply, "Is my arm too short? ... You will eat meat until it comes out your nose." He is omnipotent and can do what he wishes.

I have always known that if God created the very cells of my body, he can certainly heal that body. Does that mean that he doesn't want to heal me? Some go far as to ask if we are a toy or a form of entertainment to God. Does he toy with us like a cat playing with a mouse? This does not seem logical in light of how Jesus healed the sick and encouraged the hopeless. On one occasion Jesus even touched the leper to heal him rather than telling him to go recite a spell or to drink a potion. He didn't have to do that, but I believe he made a point to touch the untouchable and unclean because he cared for their humanity and he cared for the man who had not been touched since he had contracted leprosy.

The Greater Reality

To say that God is uncaring is not consistent with a God who would send his only begotten son "that whosoever believeth in him should not perish but have everlasting life." (John 3:16). He is present. He has the power. He cares. He cares enough to touch the leper. However, there are times when we pray for healing and there isn't any visible sign of a healing taking place. I love the story in the book of John where God healed the man by the Pool of Bethsaida. He simply told him to "get up" and it says that instantly the man was cured. The man picked up his mat and walked. It wasn't the man's amazing level of faith. He didn't even see it coming or know who Jesus was.

When I was in the hospital after my accident, my brother Ran (who is an ordained minister) called men from our church to come and pray for me. He anointed me with oil, they prayed, and ... nothing happened that anyone could see. Years later my wife and I were at a church service and those who were leading the service invited people to come forward for prayer. My wife and I went forward, and I felt a need to physically get out of my chair as a "step of faith." After all, some would argue that if a person has enough faith, God will heal them. I was held by two people as my legs hung limp underneath me. We prayed for my legs to be strengthened as I hung there. I prayed that if it was a lack of faith on my part that God would forgive my lack of faith and heal me. Eventually, when my body remained paralyzed and when no strength returned to my limbs, they helped me back into my wheelchair. Although I didn't walk out of the church that day, I felt like I had symbolically taken my "step of faith" and God's answer had been that his grace is sufficient. I needed to do it. I needed to know it wasn't because I hadn't gotten out of my chair "in faith" that I wasn't able to walk.

Many people have wanted to pray for me to be healed, and I have been glad to accept their prayers. However, I have not always gone up for prayer when there was an invitation to come forward at the end of a church service. When you go for prayer repeatedly, and you go away without being healed, it can be discouraging. I eventually have come to the conclusion that I will go if I feel led to do so, but I also don't have to go up for prayer for God to heal me. He can heal me anytime and anywhere.

But what takes more faith? Does it take more faith to believe God is good and that he is the Lord of all when he heals you with miraculous power, or does it take more faith to believe that He is still good and true when you do not receive a healing? My love for God and my love for His Son are not dependent on what he does for me. My experience has been that when people make the decision to follow Jesus and let him take charge, their lives have not always become easier but they have become better. As a matter of fact, many people have had their lives become much more difficult because they followed the Lord. When you come to know the Lord, you would rather die than turn away from him. When many of his disciples turned away from him, Jesus asked the twelve, "You don't want to leave too do you?" Peter answered him and said, "Lord, to whom would we go? You have the words of eternal life. We believe and know that you are the holy one of God."

Maybe we should be asking a different question. Should God have to explain his reasons for the things that happen to us? Maybe pain and suffering give us the ability to prove our love and devotion to God. It is easy to follow a leader when they make the decision we would have made (as if we would know what is best) or that we agree with. It is difficult to follow when we don't know the reasons for why things happen. I had "sung God's praises" when I was growing up. When I hit upon hard times I decided it was time to "Put up or shut up." Because I find it very difficult to "shut up," I decided I would continue to trust in God's goodness. As I grew up, I have always acknowledged that I have been very blessed to have grown up in a loving family, to have very good health, to have a good education, and so much more. I often wondered why I should be so blessed. I wasn't glad to experience hard times, but I knew I finally had a time to prove that I'm not a "good times believer." God knows my heart. My car accident and spinal cord injury was what helped me know my heart. Instead of looking to God to solve all of my problems, I am thankful that he lets us be a part of the process of making life better and helping those in need.

We are in a spiritual war. How we handle suffering is a testimony to others here on earth but also to those in the spiritual realm. When Job was living, the Bible described him as blameless and a man of integrity. Satan is described as the accuser and as a slanderer. He wants to steal, kill, and destroy. If he can use our suffering to distract us away from God and believe his lies about God, he will. There wasn't anything heroic about my accident. I wasn't martyred or on a missions trip or anything like that. I was too knuckle-headed to pull over even though I knew I was tired and had even dozed once already. But in another sense, Satan doesn't like us and will do anything he can to get us to question God's love for us. We need to keep in mind who the real enemy is. Satan wants to steal our joy, kill us and/or our relationships, and destroy God's plans and our families and anything that is Godly. He especially hates it when we praise God in the midst of our pain. He doesn't care if we believe in him or not. Sometimes his work is easier when we don't believe in him or acknowledge him. Satan loves it when we are self-absorbed because as long as we are building our personal kingdom we aren't building God's kingdom. He knows our personal kingdom is always a dead end.

Refined By Fire

People often tell me they don't think they could handle being a quadriplegic. I didn't know I could handle it or that I wouldn't turn from my faith, either. God knew my heart and that I could bear the load, but I needed to know it. In 1 Peter 1:6-9, Peter writes,

In this you greatly rejoice, though now for a little while you may have had to suffer grief in all kinds of trials. These have come so that your faith—of greater worth than gold, which perishes even though refined by fire—may be proved genuine and may result in praise, glory, and honor when Jesus Christ is revealed. Though you have not seen him you love him; and even though you do not see him now, you believe in him and are filled with an inexpressible and glorious joy. For you are receiving the goal of your faith, the salvation of your souls.

Hardships reveal the depth of our maturity and the depth of our love. They also protect us from becoming arrogant. The apostle Paul wrote that he experienced a "thorn in the flesh." In 2 Corinthians 12:7 he writes,

To keep me from becoming conceited because of these surpassingly great revelations, there was given me a thorn in my flesh, a messenger of Satan, to torment me. Three times I pleaded with the Lord to take it away from me. But he said to me, 'my grace is sufficient for you, for my power is made perfect in weakness.' Therefore I will boast all the more gladly about my weaknesses so that Christ's power may rest on me. That is why, for Christ's sake, I delight in weaknesses, in insults, in hardships, in persecutions, in difficulties. For when I am weak, then I am strong.

So hardship reveals the integrity of our maturity and love, and it also develops it.

Between my sophomore year of high school and my junior year I went on a 600-mile bike trip across two provinces of Canada in eight days with about sixty other people in Youth For Christ. We certainly didn't just look at each other and say,

"Hey! Let's go biking!" and jump on our bikes and head north. Not only was there a lot of planning, but we had to get our rear ends conditioned to be on a bike seat that long. We biked more miles getting ready for the trip than we did on the trip itself. Our spiritual muscles are like that as well. We don't just jump into doing the right thing or being spiritually mature. I had years of Sunday School, youth group meetings, sermons, talks with my parents, prayer, and Bible study to prepare me for the time when life would go off the road.

The struggles that I have faced have not just been to make me stronger. I have found that I can relate to others better who are going through difficulties or who have disabilities or illnesses because I have gone through hardship myself. We are to "comfort others with the comfort we have been given." How can we do that if we have not struggled? We do not have to go through the same things to relate to those who suffer. As I started a career in counseling I made it a point to tell people that I was not trying to play "problem poker" with them and say that they didn't have a right to complain in the midst of their grief because my situation or my pain was worse. If that were true then I wouldn't have anything to complain about because some people are paralyzed from their neck down. But people paralyzed from their neck down wouldn't have anything to complain about because at least they didn't have a head injury. But people with a head injury wouldn't have anything to complain about because at least they didn't die. But then dead people wouldn't have anything to complain about because at least they wouldn't have to have pimples or pay taxes, and so on and on and on. That reasoning would be ridiculous because no one would have legitimate reason to grieve about anything because someone else would have something "worse." Pain is pain whether it is emotional or physical and each person feels their own pain regardless of what someone else experiences.

When my mother passed away in 2006 from complications of diabetes, I grieved her passing even though I knew she was no longer in pain. She had been so very weak and eventually slept much of the day. My family and I rejoiced for her to be in God's presence and to be free of the struggles of this life. But I miss her and will grieve her absence until I see her again. This is why I don't think the grief process has a definitive end point. I have found peace in the midst of it over time, and I have found a way to make sense of it in my life view so that I accept it, but I'm not over my loss of her any more than I'm over the fact that I cannot do what I once was able to do.

In Philippians 3, Paul describes the difficulties he faced and how God had used his past to equip him. He writes that if anyone could boast about a resume he could. Starting in verse 7 he writes "But whatever was to my profit I now consider loss for the sake of Christ. What is more, I consider everything loss compared to the surpassing greatness of *knowing Christ Jesus* my Lord for whose sake I have lost all things. I consider them rubbish that I may gain Christ and be found in Him, not having a righteousness of my own that comes from the law but that which is through faith in Christ—the righteousness that comes from God and is by faith. I want to *know Christ* and the power of His resurrection and the fellowship of sharing in his sufferings, becoming like him in his death, and so, somehow to attain to the resurrection from the dead." If my accident resulted in me knowing the Lord better, then I rejoice that it happened.

After her family was killed for helping Jewish people and after surviving the Nazi concentration camps of WWII, Corrie ten Boom said that "There is nothing so dark or so deep that God's love is not deeper still." God loves us and has felt pain in seeing his son suffer on the cross. Christ was willing to suffer more than any of us ever will because he loves us. God was with me in the accident and with me in the hospital and with me in the loneliness in school. All that I lost is nothing compared to what I have in my relationship with God. He is eternal, and everything else I've ever had will be rust and dust. It's all going to burn one day, and the only things that will make it through are the things that I did for him.

How much do we want from God? He gave us his life and was crucified in our place. How much more do you want from him? He is giving us a hope and a future. He is reserving a place in heaven for us and God calls us his children. That is mind boggling to me. If God can use my accident to bring people to him, then so be it. Even if I had been able to play college football, I eventually would have to sit on the sidelines. Nobody plays football forever.

Today I work as a coordinator of an outpatient treatment center at St. Elizabeth's Hospital in Belleville, Illinois. It has been my privilege to come alongside of people during some of the hardest and darkest times of their life as they struggle with some of life's hardest situations. Angie and I have been married twenty-two years. She is my hero as a woman who has faithfully been by my side and encouraged me to keep fighting the good fight. I love to cook, to paint, to drive, to sing, and so much more. We are active in our church at TRWC and lead a Life Group. I also work part time counseling some of the church members in TRCC. Ashley and Amanda work and go to college and are doing well.

In rehab they warned us that scientists say that "In three to five years we will come up with a cure." But three to five years later, they are still saying, "In three to five years we will come up with a cure." It has been twenty-nine years since my accident. It is not a question for me of *If* but of *when* I will walk again. I don't care if God chooses to use a scientific breakthrough or a miracle or if he chooses to wait for the day when I meet him face to face in heaven. All I want to do when I walk again is to kneel before him and hear him say, "Well done, good and faithful servant." If God is using me and my testimony to bring people to him, then I wouldn't change a thing.

SEAN'S STORY

By the Mark Weber Family

The view from his mother, Caralee

March 1, 1988 will be forever known as the day of "Sean's Accident." This is the day that changed our lives forever, especially Sean's.

Up until then Sean's life was filled with midget league games, swimming with his friends, riding his bike, running races with his best friend and cousin Clint, going to school, and doing all the normal things a nine year old would do.

Sean has always been very outgoing. He was and still is a handsome boy. He also had a very high opinion of himself. He always said he was the best. In my opinion there's nothing wrong with that kind of thinking. Sean was a Rambo kind of character. He had long hair (about an inch or two past his shoulder), and he loved wearing headbands. Too cool of a guy to let his buddies know how much he loved his mama. That's what he called me.

He never would give me a kiss in front of the guys. Sean wasn't afraid of work: in fact, the tougher the job, the better. He loved cutting and stacking the firewood with his dad. We had a big fireplace, and we heated with wood, (did I mention we lived in Michigan?), and we used a lot of wood.

While Mark, my husband, worked at our family-owned grocery store, I worked at home, operating a horse training operation. I would break and train horses for people and then would travel around the countryside hauling their horses to competitions. Sean and his sister Tenille would have their chores to do around the barn.

Until March 1, 1988 I thought life was pretty good! We would have to make monthly trips to the grain elevator to buy oats to feed the horses, and this particular day the trip to the elevator was no different than any other trip.

We would use grain wagons to store our oats. The wagons had to be weighed at the elevator so they knew how much to charge us for the oats. By doing this we knew there was 7,700 pounds of oats in the wagon.

Once we got the grain wagon to the barn we had to maneuver it into place. It took a lot of planning and manpower to push it because the truck could only go so far into the barn with it. So the rest of the maneuvering was done by us.

We had to push the wagon off of a four-inch slab of cement onto a dirt floor, as well as turning it ninety degrees to the right.

We were just about to push it off the slab when Sean said "Wait, we have to hang up the old oak ladder first." The ladder was twelve feet long and solid oak and didn't fold up, so hanging it on the wall of the barn was the only way to store it.

I was glad Sean reminded us to hang the ladder, but I didn't really know how glad I would be later.

So there we were; everyone was in place. Even a couple of Mark's buddies from the store just happened by, so of course they were incorporated into helping with the final push. Remember, 7,700 pounds is not easy to maneuver manually.

I remember asking if everyone was out of the way.

"Where are you, Tenille?" I looked to make sure of her safety.

"Where are you, Sean?" I looked again.

Both kids seemed to be out of harm's way—or so I thought! Our lives changed forever at 5:35 pm, March 1, 1988.

Because the grain wagon was dropping off a four-inch slab of cement to a dirt floor, the wheels didn't roll off the same time. The tongue of the wagon jerked and when the tongue jerked one way, the wagon went the other way. We didn't count on that happening.

The wagon slammed against the barn wall with a loud bang. It slammed hard. I remember saying, "Wow, I can't believe the wagon didn't go right through the barn wall."

Then I remembered the old oak ladder that Sean reminded us to hang up and I think it kept the wagon with 7,700 pounds of oats from crashing through. It landed against the ladder instead.

We were quite proud of ourselves for getting this grain wagon into our barn. We were even high-fiving each other, not knowing what had happened to Sean.

While celebrating our little moving adventure, one of Mark's friends that just happened to show up for our project began to ask, "Why is Sean lying there on the ground?"

I looked quickly and ran to him and I reached for his arm and asked, "Sean, what are you doing?"

"Get up!" His arm was completely limp.

I yelled, "Oh Lord! Mark, come here! Something is wrong with Sean!"

At first I thought Sean was playing a joke on me. Oh, I wish he was!

Then when I realized that something was wrong, I cried "Oh God, please help Sean!"

Mark pulled his lifeless body out from behind the wagon.

The Greater Reality

I didn't know what happened. I saw Sean. He was out of the way of the wagon. He was way far away. How did he get hurt?

Then it came to me like a dropped rock. When the tongue of the wagon jerked, the direction of the wagon changed. It went right toward Sean and hit him!

Why wasn't he pinned against the wall? He should have been smashed. All these questions were racing through my head. The ladder, the ladder that Sean reminded us to hang on the wall, saved Sean's life.

It allowed four inches for Sean's head. I know four inches aren't a lot, but in this case it was enough.

Those four inches were enough to keep him alive!

At 5:35 pm on March 1, 1988, Sean sustained a "Closed Head Injury."

And on this day it began our journey that would last a lifetime.

The year was 1989. February! It was hard to believe a year had gone by since our son's accident. This had happened March 1, 1988. He was nine years old. Just a little over a month away from his tenth birthday. A lot was going on then. Mark was working at our family owned business, a grocery store, putting in sixty-plus hours a week.

Mark had a lot of guilt, putting in all those hours at the time because that meant the bulk of the traveling back and forth to hospitals and rehab facilities rested with me. Also, Tenille, who was twelve at the time was going through a tough time dealing with the loss of the brother who was her closest ally, and realizing that he would never be the same, again. She also, unbeknownst to us, had experienced some abuse and kept that bottled up also, because Mark and I had been so wrapped up with Sean that she felt alone. We found out later that it was at this time she began experimenting with drugs and alcohol to escape her unpleasant reality. With

Mark working a lot, Tenille withdrawn into herself: and Sean unable to communicate, I felt pretty much alone.

We lived about a two-and-one-half hour drive away from the rehab facility where Sean was at the time. I would make the drive every other day and stay pretty much the whole day. I wanted to be there to make sure Sean was not alone and was getting the treatment he was supposed to be receiving. While driving back and forth to see Sean, I would pray for Sean's recovery—for him to be able to walk, talk, and be the boy I remembered. I would cry every time I left him. I was really missing "my Sean." I had had a very close relationship with him. I didn't have one regret about the past, but I had one selfish desire. I wanted my "old Sean" back. Looking back, I was becoming very depressed, maybe even suicidal. I was feeling alone, like there was no one I could turn to.

Sean's head trauma had been severe, he wasn't expected to live, but when he did make it through the critical stages and finally was able to leave the ICU, we were not left with much hope about his long-term prognosis. We felt God saved Sean for a reason, and we tried to keep our hopes high for the future, praying constantly and looking for any sign of improvement. But several doctors time and again would dash our hopes with cruel words of discouragement. This was our predicament at the time. I needed a sign. I needed something to happen to give me the strength I required to keep on going.

In June 1989, the people at Sean's rehabilitation facility were planning a day at the Kent County Youth Fair for the patients. I volunteered to be a chaperone. Of course, my plan was just to take care of Sean and make sure he got to see as much as possible. I am sorry if that sounds selfish.

It was a beautiful day. The bus pulled up into the parking lot and all the kids from the group, (most in wheelchairs like Sean) were taken off the buses and assigned to their chaperones. They were promptly wheeled into a little park area by picnic tables, but I was long gone with Sean. We came to see

The Greater Reality

the fair. And, we were going to do it. We started in the 4-H cow barn and watched the cow judging. We even had some of the kids come over to meet Sean, and they brought their cows over to show Sean up close. Man, they were big.

We wandered through the exhibit buildings taking it all in and then we eventually ended up down the midway. We reminisced about all the fond memories of experiences at past trips to fair midways. Our kids had been involved in showing horses at county fairs for several years before Sean's accident. Sean had always loved the midway rides, especially roller coaster-type rides. I decided to look here for one. Sure enough before long I found one. It was a "kiddie coaster,' by no means a thriller like at the amusement parks, but that was okay, we just came to watch it.

You see, Sean was bound in to his specially adapted wheelchair, complete with straps and harnesses, and even a helmet he wore that was kind of bungee-corded to the chair to stabilize his head. At that time he was unable to bold his own head up for more than a few seconds at a time.

So there we were in front of the ride, Sean in his bizarre looking get up and me kneeling down next to him talking to him about the ride, waiting to watch some other kids ride, but strangely enough the ride was empty and there wasn't even anyone in line. I thought, too bad Sean can't ride it, there's no waiting.

But when I studied the mounting platform, with its seven steps and looked at Sean. I thought it might as well be Mount Everest. Then a voice said, "Do you want to ride?"

I looked up and a young man was standing there. I said, "Thank you, but I don't see how we can. Sean can't walk and he doesn't have much head control. I don't know if he could handle it even if I could get him on the ride."

While I was telling him about the obstacles, I noticed while looking at the young man that he didn't seem to be your typical "carny." I don't mean to be judgmental, but I had been to a lot of carnivals and the attendants at most of them usually were a pretty scruffy-looking bunch. But this young man was clean cut, had on clean orange overalls, and just had an air about him that didn't fit with the typical image. My mind whirled with thoughts. How can Sean do this? The doctors and therapists all kept telling me that Sean can't live a normal life. They said that the best thing for him and us was to institutionalize him. Here I am considering putting him on a roller coaster! Am I insane?

Then the young man said "I'll help you. You take one side, I'll take the other and we'll walk him up the stairs to the platform. Then you get in the car and I'll lift him in to you."

I didn't know if Sean could walk with our help. Until then the most we had ever done with him is get him to stand with someone supporting him and then just for a few seconds. But with this young man's help we got Sean up those steps and into the car. I put one arm around his chest and supported the back of his head with the other arm. Hopefully this would stabilize his head because I was doubtful about him being able to hold it still. I was scared.

The young man said "I'll watch you closely all the way around. If Sean has any trouble, hold up your hand and I'll stop the coaster immediately, and we'll get him out."

Still, during the whole time it took us to board the coaster, nobody else had gotten in line to ride. We were the only two on the whole ride. He started us off real slow. I was so scared. I kept thinking what if something happens to Sean up here? What if he gets over stimulated and has a seizure? Please God help me! Then Sean just came alive on that coaster. He smiled, then he laughed out loud. He screamed in the dips and turns. I lost my fear. I was laughing for joy at Sean's reactions to the ride. It had been so long since I've seen any kind of excitement on his face like this. Still no other people had shown up for the ride. The attendant let us ride it four times in a row! By the time we were finished, I no longer had to

The Greater Reality

hold Sean's head up. He was doing it by himself. The young man came over to us.

I said "I think we'd better get off now. We've been gone a long time from the rest of the group and I don't want them to come looking for us and find out what we have done, and report it to the doctors and therapists at the rehab facility."

So we got Sean off the same way we got on: one of us on each side, coaching him on taking one step at a time with each leg down the stairs. Then he helped me get Sean back in the wheelchair and strapped in.

Still, in all the time this took, no one else had walked up to the ride. I took out the tickets I had in my pocket and knew it wasn't enough to cover the four rides we had taken. The young man just said "I don't want any of your tickets. I'm just glad I got to help give him this experience." I thanked him over and over again. The young man was so nice to Sean. He knelt down and touched Sean's knee and said "It was nice to meet you, Sean."

I turned and wheeled Sean away with tears in my eyes. I said "Sean, wasn't that great? I can hardly believe it, you rode a roller coaster!"

I stopped to turn around once more to yell thanks to the young man. But to my shock, he was gone.

There was a different guy running the ride. And not only that, but there was probably about forty to fifty people now lined up at the queue. At that moment, I knew God was behind this. I believe God had sent an angel in the being of this young man to give me the sign I needed to go on. He showed me that life could go on for Sean and us. That nothing was going to stop us from living and enjoying a normal life, with everything there is to experience and savor.

God also showed me something else. Sean was going to get better. But not in rehabs with doctors and therapists who only stressed what Sean couldn't do. No, Sean was going to get better with our family doing the therapy and

God directing us. God came to show me this, that at the Kent County Youth Fair.

Post Script
Twenty years have passed, and we have since sold everything and moved to Florida. Sean is now thirty-one years old. He still lives with us and although he continues to live with disabilities, he is a very happy and soulful individual who lives and loves life everyday like we all should.

The view from his father, Mark
Sean was less than two months short of his tenth birthday on the day of his accident, March 1, 1988. He had been chewed out by his mother earlier that afternoon for eating four bakery-fresh cream-filled pastries after coming home from school. But when I came home from the store that night, there he was as always, waiting to help me in the barn with chores. Sean was always a big help for his age. Ever since he was old enough to work, he would follow me around, wanting to do whatever I was doing, especially if it was "man's work." Building stalls, mending fence, splitting wood, and mowing the lawn were all jobs he wanted to be involved in. Just a few months earlier, I came home in the wee hours of the morning from a band job expecting to have to unload a wagon of hay in the barn before I went to bed, only to discover an empty wagon and neatly stacked hay waiting for me in the barn. Sean had done it all by himself because his mother was sick and unable to do it.

He was all boy, rough and ready, but with a tender side to him. He was always close to his mama and would sit with her and watch the ice skating competition on the televised Winter Games that year, giving his own running commentary on each skater's performance. He was also a pretty good artist for his age, a talent he obviously inherited from his mama.

The Greater Reality

We have kept some of his work from those days, and even have a framed picture of a cardinal he did as a seven year old.

Sean was a thoughtful boy who really displayed selflessness sometimes. One story I like to tell is of the time he was at weekend horse show with his mother and sister. Sean was not into horses like they were, but he was always there for them, watching the contest and helping with the horses. That particular weekend was over the Memorial Day Holiday, and as was the case quite often, I wasn't there with them, staying home to work.

There was a flea market at the fairgrounds where the horse show was, and Sean was browsing the vendor tables while the horse show was going on. At the time, I had a stein collection of sorts. Well, Sean had spied a stein at one of the tables that he was sure I would like. He went back to find his mother and told her about it and said that he would like to buy it for me as Father's Day gift. Caralee told him she would go with him after she was done showing for the day and check it out. About four hours later, she went over to the flea market and found Sean standing by the table with the stein display.

The vendor asked her, "Is this your boy?

She answered that he was and hoped he had not been any trouble.

The vendor smiled and said, "Do you know that boy stood guard over the stein all afternoon? Every time any customer got anywhere near the stein, he would pick it up, pretend to examine it until they moved on. He wasn't going to let anyone get that stein."

Needless to say, although I've long gotten rid of the rest of my stein collection, that one still remains in my possession and will till I'm gone.

After Sean's accident, I used to wonder how he would have turned out as the years went by. When the boys in his class were playing high school football, when his classmates graduated from high school, and even when his old friends went on to college and got married to begin their families, I wondered. When Sean suffered his accident, I was tortured by the thought would he be aware of the loss of his physical and mental abilities? I prayed earnestly to God that if this was to be Sean's plight in life, that he be spared the memory of how he used to be so he wouldn't suffer from the knowledge of his disability.

God has answered my prayer, because either Sean is unaware of his loss, or he is aware but has been blessed with that peace that surpasses all understanding that the Apostle Paul talked about, because he is one of the happiest and most contented people I know. He is a daily example to me of how we are to approach life, not in judgment of our existence as being good or bad, but thankful and happy just to be alive at all.

The author of this book would like to share the following thought with you. The attitude of the Weber family is expressed wonderfully by a slogan above a doorway in their home.

"Life is not waiting for the storm to end; life is about learning to dance in the rain."

They have found the truth and validity of several verses in the Scriptures:

> ... be content with what you have, because God has said, "Never will I leave you; never will I forsake you."
>
> So we say with confidence, "The Lord is my helper; I will not be afraid. What can man do to me?"
>
> Hebrews 13:5b-6 (NIV)
>
> I will not leave you as orphans; I will come to you.
> John 14:18 (NIV)

I can do everything through him who gives me strength. Philippians 4:13 (NIV)

The Weber family accepts without question the thoughts if David in the twenty-third Psalm:

A Psalm of David

The Lord is my shepherd, I shall not be in want.
He makes me lie down in green pastures, he leads me beside quiet waters, he restores my soul.
He guides me in paths of righteousness for his name's sake.
Even though I walk through the valley of the shadow of death, I will fear no evil, for you are with me; your rod and your staff, they comfort me.
You prepare a table before me in the
presence of my enemies.
You anoint my head with oil; my cup overflows.
Surely goodness and love will follow me all the days of my life, and I will dwell in the house of the Lord forever. (Psalm 23 NIV)

The Weber family are living examples of "lives of gratitude" lived out before us. They are great inspirations to all who are privileged to know them.

CAROL

Carol was born into a Christian home where she learned what true love is. She was taught both the love for God and the love we are to have for one another. These lessons were taught not only by written word, but by lives of faithful witnesses lived out before her—a rich heritage from parents, grandparents, aunts, and uncles. Not knowing that not everyone is raised that way, she took it for granted that that was the life she could make.

As so many women who lived before her, it was her desire to find the "right" man, marry him, and be the loving, faithful wife and mother that she knew God wanted her to be. Believing that she had found that person, she married him But, Carol was not long into the marriage before she knew that the one she had married had no idea of what true love and faithfulness were. After a few short years of struggling in an abusive relationship, she tried six times to repair her marriage, but finally was left on her own to provide for and raise three small boys. She went through a time of struggle, including depression while trying to deal with the hand she had been given.

But the foundations of faith with which she had been raised kicked in. In the words of her father, "She took the lemon she had been given, and made lemonade out of it." She enrolled in college, received a CETA grant, made do with what she had, and got her degree as a registered nurse. Carol entered a field where she could help others with her education and training, and she has spent her life doing just that.

When her sons were grown she opened her home to foster children. Over sixty children have lived in her home. She was sure that if she could show them that there were choices and that it was their responsibility to choose how to live their lives, that she would make a difference. She felt that once they were shown the love of Jesus that they would choose him. In all the years we have known her, she has had a victorious and buoyant spirit. Her approach to life is, "God has not failed me, and God is not going to fail me. God doesn't make mistakes. He creates you to be the individual you are, not perfect, but His." She lives a life of gratitude, continually sharing how good God has been to her.

Carol is a living example to all who know her that it is not the circumstances of life that ultimately control one's destiny; it is what you do with those circumstances that make all the difference in the world.

There are several verses that Carol's "Attitude of Gratitude" bring to mind.

> I can do everything through him who gives me strength. Philippians 4:13 (NIV)

> I know what it is to be in need, and I know what it is to have plenty. I have learned the secret of being content in any and every situation, whether well fed or hungry, whether living in plenty or in want. I can do everything through him who gives me strength. (Philippians 4:12-13 NIV)

> The Lord is my shepherd, I shall not be in want.
> He makes me lie down in green pastures, he leads me beside quiet waters, he restores my soul.

He guides me in paths of righteousness for his name's sake.
Even though I walk through the valley of the shadow of death, I will fear no evil,
for you are with me; your rod and your staff, they comfort me.
You prepare a table before me in the presence of my enemies.
You anoint my head with oil; my cup overflows.
Surely goodness and love will follow me all the days of my life, and I will dwell in the house of the Lord forever. (Psalm 23 NIV)

David said, "Because The Lord is my shepherd, I shall not be in want," and he also said, "Even though I walk through the valley of the shadow of death, I will fear no evil." Carol knew the truth of this. She knows it now. It is what carries her through every day. With her attitude of gratitude, Carol looks forward to that day when she shall hear her Savior say: "'Well done, good and faithful servant! You have been faithful with a few things; I will put you in charge of many things. Come and share your master's happiness'" (Matthew 25:21 NIV)!

So if God would give her a ranch out in the middle of nowhere, she wanted an alternative to incarceration for people with drug and alcohol addictions. She would create a loving home where they could find the answers they are seeking and find the love of God that can change lives.

An Addendum by Carol:

I would like for you to read a paper I wrote earlier entitled, "Jesus Loves Me" with the subtitle "Anger from a Mother's Point of View," by Carol Loy Morgan. It is my prayer that it will give some mother new faith and hope.

Jesus does love me, but at first I thought it was because I was a Loy. I was raised in the church where everybody loved my family and me. I was one of seven Loy children—my grandfather was pastor of the church I was raised in before we lived there.

Sometimes I felt lost in the chaos of seven children in a big family. I helped my dad and mom build a four-bedroom house in the country by keeping the four younger brothers and sisters in town while my brother and sister did the actual pounding nails. I was twelve and thirteen years old that year. When I was seventeen, I realized that Jesus loved me just for me and that he had a plan for my life.

Jeremiah 1:4-5 states, "The word of the Lord came to me saying "Before I formed you in the womb I knew you. Before you were born I set you apart."

When I was nineteen I started nursing classes at Michigan State University in a class of 2000, but they only accept eighty into their sophomore class, so I gave up easily and married Jim. He told me that no one else would ever love me like he loved me. The first year we moved to Fort Lauderdale, Florida, because of the work situation in Michigan where there were lay-offs of thousands from the car industry. I was isolated away from my family with no car, but I found a church close by that I could walk to.

We returned to Michigan after Tom was born, when Jim's mother was diagnosed with breast cancer. I had three sons in four years and became convinced that something I had done caused our relationship to become abusive. We divorced and I returned to college at St. Clair County Community College and completed my Associate degree in Nursing by 1980 when my youngest wasn't yet two years old. I tried to mend my relationship with Jim six times in the next six years. Each time he'd have a different reason why it would work out—he had a job, he wasn't drinking anymore, on and on. I finally quit trying after my oldest had to dial 911 when his daddy was hurting me.

I finally moved to New Mexico in 1986 to leave the abuse behind. I've been an RN for twenty-eight years. I've involved my children in church, including Sunday School, Bible school, church camp, Boy Scouts, 4-H, Tae Kwan Do, and vacations home to Michigan and South Dakota. I had brought them up right, after the violence ended, or so I thought.

In 2001 my second son, Kris, and I were working on his truck. I was handing him tools and parts from the trunk of my Grand Prix when the Region 5 drug task force, dressed in Black Kevlar vests and black ski masks came running down the sidewalk in front of his house yelling "Get on the Ground! Get on the Ground!"

I didn't understand what was happening. I just backed away from them looking at my son and his friend with their hands on the ground in front of them lying face down on the pavement. One of the sheriff's deputies came up from the other direction, and I asked him what was going on and he looked down at Kris. I could see the light bulb go on in his head, "Morgan."

I could tell by the look on his face that they were after Kris. They never did make me get on the ground, search me, or my car. They all knew me. But they took Kris to jail after searching his house. They found a roommate's drug paraphernalia, and Kris served two years in prison because the lease on the house was in his name. They had been watching his house because they thought he was dealing drugs.

It turned out to be a good thing. He had been on drugs. He received the Lord as his Savior in prison, came back to the Portales jail, and he went through rehab at the Step House in Alamagordo following the prison time. From there he moved to Roswell and opened his own step house—helping dozens of guys get clean and sober. He became the manager at Jiffy Lube for three and a half years.

He took on a wife and her five children. He became a great daddy. He was so successful in his business that he thought he could open his own car repair business in Fort Sumner, but he was not very good at collecting money, and people there quickly took advantage of that. He became frustrated and depressed when he wasn't making any money before Christmas last year. He started working with my oldest son, Tom in construction and when the construction job in Fort Sumner was finished he came back to Portales. His old cronies quickly got him involved in drugs again, and he was arrested in May for nondrug related charges.

Should I be angry? If I was I would rave at God! Why didn't You protect him? Why didn't the hedge of protection I prayed for every day keep him from harming himself and his family?

That's not my God—he didn't cause Kris to make bad choices, and each time bad things happened, I could see His hand at work. I see Kris growing as a man. He is using his witness for Christ right now in jail. He wasn't going to church in Fort Sumner. He wasn't giving Christ control of his life.

Matthew 7:9 says, "Which of you, if his son asks for bread, will give him a stone? Or if he asks for a fish, will give him a snake? If you then, who are evil, know how to give good gifts to your children How much more will your father in heaven give good gifts to those who ask him."

I know that God has given Kris a pastor in jail right now from the Cowboy Church who has given him a Bible and good material to read while he's in jail. I am sure God has his attention and is growing him in ways I can't see. He is also giving him opportunities to witness to people he might not reach on the streets of life.

Please join me in praying for Kris, Andrea, Carlos, Nate, Kayla, Noah, and Jacob. I'm hoping they will be reunited soon.

FINDING THE GREATER REALITY

The first step toward living in victory, possessing that greater reality, is to settle the question of the reality of God. I will deal with that question first. I have shared a few stories of people who were caught in a reality that we could see with our naked eyes. But, they possessed another reality which we could not see that gave them victory over the reality we were seeing. These are witnesses. The Apostle Paul said that we are surrounded by witnesses.

> Therefore, since we are surrounded by such a great cloud of witnesses, let us throw off everything that hinders and the sin that so easily entangles, and let us run with perseverance the race marked out for us. Let us fix our eyes on Jesus, the author and perfecter of our faith, who for the joy set before him endured the cross, scorning its shame, and sat down at the right hand of the throne of God. (Hebrews 12:1-3 NIV)

Paul was referring here to those who have gone on before who he seems to suggest watch, at least in part, our race of life. I would suggest that there are other witnesses. God allows us to see the witnesses to the truth of his promises to us. These are witnesses who lived with unseen realities that carried them victoriously over visible realities, which were devastation to others who experienced the same thing in their lives. What made the difference?

First, they believed in the living God of creation. They believed in the God who is Lord of life. The Apostle Paul said, "For since the creation of the world God's invisible qualities—his eternal power and divine nature—have been clearly seen, being understood from what has been made, so that men are without excuse" (Romans 1:20 NIV). Paul is exactly right. Those who choose to ignore God are without excuse. The evidence of God is all around us.

In a psychology textbook *Child Development* the following passage introduces the subject: "One cell from the man and one cell from the woman unite and make one cell. Never again are any cells ever added. The mother's body nourishes the cell until it grows and divides. She nourishes the two until they grow and divide. And never again are any cells ever added." Nine months later, from one cell we have the most automated machine the world has ever seen. From one cell we have eye balls, nerves, muscles, bone structure, skin, the various organs, a brain, heart, lungs, kidneys, and all the rest. No one will ever convince me that all that is an accident.

Science with all its mathematical exactness tells us that when you go out into the dark at night and look up into the blue, you are looking into infinity. Science says that there is no other side to the blue you are looking into. Science tells us that every time they get a stronger telescope, the more stars they can see that they never saw before. Every star is a solar system. All held in perfect balance.

Think about this liquid egg we live on. Science tells us that it is twenty-five thousand miles around, and the crust is about fourteen miles thick. Go straight down fourteen miles, and it begins to turn to liquid. That is not very thick for a globe that measures twenty-five thousand miles in circumference. It turns once every twenty-four hours. So those on the equator are moving through space at better than a thousand miles per hour. Yet, we feel no vibration. Small wonder we have an earthquake every once in a awhile.

There are many other things we could take the time to share, but it is not necessary.

The Evolutionary theory has some truth. It is my belief that God may have used a number of processes of evolvement in the process of creation. But, believing in evolution as the heart and core of creation is to leave great unanswered questions. Two large questions produce pause for reflection for me. In the process of evolving, why do we still have monkeys as they have always been, while others became, over a period of time, humans? Why do some remain totally as they were?

My second question is, what put into the very first single cell the drive to become something better? To put it another way, why do things progress upward instead of regressing in a backward direction? Where did the desire to improve come from for that first single cell?

The evidence that God is intimately involved: Do you accept it? But the answer to that question is the same as answering the question of the resurrection of Jesus Christ. Someone once said that you could prove the resurrection of Jesus Christ by simply reasoning with the facts involved. Let me explain.

Many years ago, someone stated that you could have divided the crowds gathered in Jerusalem that long-ago day into three categories. There were those who hated Jesus. There were the indifferent ones, and there were Jesus' friends. We do have written records representing all three groups that were represented that day. We have the writings of the enemies of Jesus, the writings of a neutral witness, and the writings of the friends of Jesus.

First there were the writings of the enemies of Jesus, the leadership of the organized church of the day. Inside the door of the synagogue in Jerusalem scribes sat at a table

The Greater Reality

twenty-four hours a day, seven days a week. It was the task of the one sitting there to write down everything that occurred which affected the life of the temple in any way. That running account was known as the "Talmud." That weekend, it was recorded in this record, the Talmud, that a carpenter, Jesus of Nazareth, was crucified on a cross on Golgotha on Friday afternoon. He was taken down and buried in a tomb by sunset. Sunday morning that tomb was empty.

We have the writings of the neutral witness. Rome had an appointed recorder directed to record everything that occurred which involved the Roman Army in any manner. This man's name was Josephus. He was directly ordered to record accurately everything that occurred involving the army of Rome in any way. His orders included a mandate that the records were to be accurate. His record is the same as the Talmud. Josephus wrote that a carpenter, Jesus of Nazareth, was crucified on a cross on Golgotha on Friday afternoon. He was taken down and buried in a tomb by sunset. And again, Sunday morning that tomb was empty.

Then there are the written records of the friends of Jesus. We know these four records as the Gospels. Once again, they record in these records that Jesus of Nazareth was crucified on a cross on Golgotha on Friday afternoon. He was taken down and buried in a tomb by sunset. And, Sunday morning that tomb was empty.

The written accounts that we have from that day all agree to this point. Jesus was crucified, dead, and buried, and on the third day the tomb was empty. It is only at this point that they disagree. Examine what we have so far. Then ask the question, how was the tomb emptied?

Break it down. To do that we recall that the crowds in Jerusalem that day could be divided into three groups: the enemies, the neutral bystanders, and the friends of Jesus. Did the enemies of Jesus take the body? That makes no sense. They would have done everything in their power to destroy this new faith in the next few years. This new faith, known as "The Way," was based and centered on a "Risen Christ." All they would have had to do to destroy this new movement was produce a body. No, you cannot go with that explanation.

How about the neutral bystanders? Every crowd that gathers has within it a group of people, probably the largest group, who are along for the ride. They will shout "Hosanna" on Sunday, but change their cries to "Crucify" on Thursday. They just want to be a part of the things that were happening. Mostly, they loved to be entertained. Was it possible that these who were along for the ride stole the body as a prank? Probably not! Roman soldiers were given orders to succeed or die. The reason that Rome was so successful on the battlefield was that the armies of Rome went into battle under an order to win or die. Roman soldiers who lost in battle were executed. There was a Roman contingent present at the tomb under those same orders, so I doubt seriously if pranksters stole the body.

How about the friends of Jesus? This is the place where the Talmud differs from the other records. The Talmud says, "His friends stole the body." If that were true, these were some of the world's most naive people. Over the next several years some of them will die for their faith. Others will watch loved ones die. What will they die for? A risen Lord and Savior that they know did not rise from the grave? No, the only answer you can come up with that makes sense is that the body arose on its own. But let me hasten to share this. If that is all the proof you have, you do not have enough proof.

The only proof that is life-changing is when you know him face to face. The only proof worth having is a personal relationship with Jesus Christ. When God is real because you walk with Him, and you talk with him, then you know that there is a God. Yes! Let God happen to you.

Now what? Let's understand the nature of that God. How does God feel about you?

THE NATURE OF GOD

The Bible is all about one subject: "covenant." God wants to have a relationship with you. In the very beginning of God's Word, we are told that God created man and woman in his own image. The creator wanted a relationship with his creation. It was a natural thing for God to walk and talk with his creation. Look at the following verse. "Then the man and his wife heard the sound of the LORD God as he was walking in the garden in the cool of the day, and they hid from the LORD God among the trees of the garden. But the LORD God called to the man, "Where are you" (Genesis 3:8-9 NIV)? Yes, God created humankind for fellowship with Himself.

The act of rebelliousness and disobedience broke that fellowship. But God wanted that relationship restored. He saved Noah and his family, then made them a promise: "Then God said to Noah and to his sons with him: "I now establish my covenant with you and with your descendants after you and with every living creature that was with you—the birds, the livestock and all the wild animals, all those that came out of the ark with you—every living creature on earth" (Genesis 9:8-10 NIV).

He renewed his covenant again with Abram and changed his name to Abraham.

> I will establish my covenant as an everlasting covenant between me and you and your descendants after you for the generations to come, to be your God and the God of your descendants after you. (Genesis 17:7 NIV)

> Then God said to Abraham, "As for you, you must keep my covenant, you and your descendants after you for the generations to come. (Genesis 17:9 NIV)

He made the first covenant with Noah because Noah was a righteous man in the midst of an unrighteous people.

God made the covenant with Abraham because Abraham believed him enough to take Him at his word.

"Abram believed the Lord, and he credited it to him as righteousness" (Genesis 15:6 NIV). That faith was so important that God had it placed in His Word again three times roughly twenty centuries later. What does Scripture say? "And the scripture was fulfilled that says, "Abraham believed God, and it was credited to him as righteousness," and he was called God's friend" (James 2:23; see also Romans 4:3; Galatians 3:6; NIV)..

It is worth noting that the phrase "and he was called God's friend" was added. That phrase is tied to the statement "Abraham believed God."

God next renewed the covenant with Isaac: "Then God said, "Yes, but your wife Sarah will bear you a son, and you will call him Isaac. I will establish my covenant with him as an everlasting covenant for his descendants after him (Genesis 17:19 NIV), and with Jacob:

> There above it stood the LORD, and he said: "I am the LORD, the God of your father Abraham and the God of Isaac. I will give you and your descendants the land on which you are lying. Your descendants will

be like the dust of the earth, and you will spread out to the west and to the east, to the north and to the south. All peoples on earth will be blessed through you and your offspring. I am with you and will watch over you wherever you go, and I will bring you back to this land. I will not leave you until I have done what I have promised you." (Genesis 28:13-15 NIV)

God referred to the covenant he made with Abraham, Isaac, and Jacob when He began working with Moses.

We need to remember that in its simplest form, God's covenant was, is, and always will be: I will be your God, and you will be my people. As I have observed people throughout my years of ministry, it is my conclusion that God has always done His part in the keeping of the covenant. The problem comes in with our being able to understand and consistently be "His people."

God faithfully continued, "God also said to Moses, 'Say to the Israelites, 'The LORD, the God of your fathers—the God of Abraham, the God of Isaac and the God of Jacob—has sent me to you'" (Exodus 3:15 NIV).

After God had guided the Children of Israel out of Egypt, he had Moses come up on Mount Sinai. "The LORD said to Moses, 'Come up to me on the mountain and stay here, and I will give you the tablets of stone with the law and commandments I have written for their instruction'" (Exodus 24:15 NIV). Moses was on the mountain a long time, receiving instruction from the Lord on the keeping of the covenant. "Then Moses entered the cloud as he went on up the mountain. And he stayed on the mountain forty days and forty nights" (Exodus 24:18 NIV). "When the LORD finished speaking to Moses on Mount Sinai, he gave him the two tablets of the covenant law, the tablets of stone inscribed by the finger of

God" (Exodus 31:18 NIV). Those instructions fill chapters 25–31 of The Book of Exodus.

A major problem that the Children of Israel had in keeping the covenant was that a great portion of their response to God was based on fear rather than love. By the time Jesus came, they had multiplied the original list of Ten Commandments to over six hundred rules for living. One wonders sometimes why they did not think to substitute for "Commandments" words like, truths, principles, or ten answers to the question, "What does it take to have fellowship with God?" Anyway, the keeping of their "rules for living" structure had become a maddening maze of impossibility. It was the question of the entire crowd that day when the lawyer asked,

> One of them, an expert in the law, tested him with this question: 'Teacher, which is the greatest commandment in the Law?'
>
> Jesus replied: 'Love the Lord your God with all your heart and with all your soul and with all your mind.' This is the first and greatest commandment. And the second is like it: 'Love your neighbor as yourself.' All the Law and the Prophets hang on these two commandments.' (Matthew 22:35-40 NIV)

When one examines that statement in the light of the Ten Commandments, one sees a harmony. The first four commandments have to do with the vertical relationship, our relationship with God. The last six have to do with what I call our "horizontal" relationships, our relationships with those around us with whom we share this road of life. I believe they are tied together in one commandment because the horizontal relationships are direct indicators of how well we are doing with our vertical relationship. The truth is, when the horizontal relationships are not right, it is because the vertical relationship is not right.

When Jesus concluded His statement with, "All the Law and the Prophets hang on these two commandments," He was sharing that when we receive, understand, and obey these two, the rest naturally fall into place. When a person loves God first and neighbor as self, the keeping of the rest of the structure is a natural result. Accepting the greatest commandment, we need to emphasize one other point.

Regarding the law, Jesus said,

> Do not think that I have come to abolish the Law or the Prophets; I have not come to abolish them but to fulfill them. For truly I tell you, until heaven and earth disappear, not the smallest letter, not the least stroke of a pen, will by any means disappear from the Law until everything is accomplished. Therefore anyone who sets aside one of the least of these commands and teaches others accordingly will be called least in the kingdom of heaven, but whoever practices and teaches these commands will be called great in the kingdom of heaven. For I tell you that unless your righteousness surpasses that of the Pharisees and the teachers of the law, you will certainly not enter the kingdom of heaven. (Matthew 5:17-20 NIV)

What Jesus said about the greatest commandment did not replace the law which had been given. It, in fact, gave new and deeper meaning to the law. Examine the concluding sentence of this passage: "For I tell you that unless your righteousness surpasses that of the Pharisees and the teachers of the law, you will certainly not enter the kingdom of heaven" (Matthew 5:20 NIV). When our obedience to the law in the fulfilling of what Jesus said was the greatest commandment springs forth from and because of our love and gratitude for what God did for us through Jesus Christ on the cross, then our righteousness surpasses the Pharisees and the teachers of the law at that point. Too often they kept and obeyed the law through fear of God rather than love and because of admiration and love of the law itself rather than the one who gave the law.

In love with God, we invite Jesus Christ into our hearts to be both Savior and Lord. He is either both Savior and Lord or he is neither one. You can have obedience without love. There are those who obey because they are afraid not to. But, you cannot claim to love without obedience. To love Him is to obey Him.

> "If you love me, keep my commands. And I will ask the Father, and he will give you another advocate to help you and be with you forever—the Spirit of truth. The world cannot accept him, because it neither sees him nor knows him. But you know him, for he lives with you and will be in you. I will not leave you as orphans; I will come to you. Before long, the world will not see me anymore, but you will see me. Because I live, you also will live. On that day you will realize that I am in my Father, and you are in me, and I am in you. Whoever has my commands and keeps them is the one who loves me. The one who loves me will be loved by my Father, and I too will love them and show myself to them."
>
> Then Judas (not Judas Iscariot) said, "But, Lord, why do you intend to show yourself to us and not to the world?"
> Jesus replied, "Anyone who loves me will obey my teaching. My Father will love them, and we will come to them and make our home with them. Anyone who does not love me will not obey my teaching. These

The Greater Reality

words you hear are not my own; they belong to the Father who sent me. (John 14:15-24 NIV)

Notice that three times in this page Jesus equates love and obedience as being one. Verse 15 says, "If you love me, keep my commands." Then verse 21a says, "Whoever has my commands and keeps them is the one who loves me." Again, in verse 23, Jesus replied, "Anyone who loves me will obey my teaching." Based on that obedience, to those Jesus says, "My Father will love them, and we will come to them and make our home with them." Then Jesus repeats this theme in reverse in verse 24, "Anyone who does not love me will not obey my teaching. ' And then Jesus emphasizes the validity of these verses with: "These words you hear are not my own; they belong to the Father who sent me."

With the above as our background, let us now note the two marching orders Jesus gave to those who would follow Him. The first, we call "the love" marching order: "A new command I give you: Love one another. As I have loved you, so you must love one another. By this everyone will know that you are my disciples, if you love one another" (John 13:34-35 NIV). It is interesting to note here that Jesus skips many of the things we in the church world might have thought were very necessary in our walk: great missionary programs, Bible studies, stained glass windows, lettered pastors, piety, and so forth. We will be known in the secular and religious world as being His by our love, period!

The absolutely best scriptural source I believe to be the most revealing of what it means to live out that love with the entire world, beginning at our own doorstep is Matthew's Gospel, chapter Twenty Five. Jesus Himself is speaking. It has always been my conviction that when Jesus spoke, we need to pay attention. He is speaking about end times and final things in this chapter. It is well worth noting, and paying special attention to one's personal walk of faith as we read.

> "When the Son of Man comes in his glory, and all the angels with him, he will sit on his glorious throne. All the nations will be gathered before him, and he will separate the people one from another as a shepherd separates the sheep from the goats. He will put the sheep on his right and the goats on his left."
>
> "Then the King will say to those on his right, 'Come, you who are blessed by my Father; take your inheritance, the kingdom prepared for you since the creation of the world. For I was hungry and you gave me something to eat, I was thirsty and you gave me something to drink, I was a stranger and you invited me in, I needed clothes and you clothed me, I was sick and you looked after me, I was in prison and you came to visit me.'
>
> "Then the righteous will answer him, 'Lord, when did we see you hungry and feed you, or thirsty and give you something to drink? When did we see you a stranger and invite you in, or needing clothes and clothe you? When did we see you sick or in prison and go to visit you?'
>
> "The King will reply, 'Truly I tell you, whatever you did for one of the least of these brothers and sisters of mine, you did for me.'
>
> "Then he will say to those on his left, 'Depart from me, you who are cursed, into the eternal fire prepared for the devil and his angels. For I was hungry and you gave me nothing to eat, I was thirsty and you

gave me nothing to drink, I was a stranger and you did not invite me in, I needed clothes and you did not clothe me, I was sick and in prison and you did not look after me.'

"They also will answer, 'Lord, when did we see you hungry or thirsty or a stranger or needing clothes or sick or in prison, and did not help you?'"

"He will reply, 'Truly I tell you, whatever you did not do for one of the least of these, you did not do for me.'

"Then they will go away to eternal punishment, but the righteous to eternal life." (Matthew 25:31-46 NIV)

A very interesting incident took place the last time I preached on this passage while still under appointment to the local church and prior to becoming a superintendent. It had always been my practice, just after I read the passage where Jesus said he would divide those before him as a shepherd divides the sheep from the goats to stop and make the following statement. "When I get to heaven, I want to ask why sheep were arbitrarily good while goats were arbitrarily bad."

Following the service that day, a visiting rancher remained and said he really enjoyed the service, and then asked if he could share with me something about my sermon.

I said, "Of course."

He asked if I had ever worked with sheep or goats. I replied that I had worked one time with some sheep, but never with goats. He said, "Pastor, I have both animals on my ranch up north of here. Sheep will follow you wherever you lead them. Sheep are obedient. You have to pen them up to keep them from following you.

Goats, you cannot even drive them. They will fight you every step of the way."

He pointed out that today in the Middle East, they still work with sheep the same as they did back then. Every family at that time, as many of them still do today, had sheep. Especially to Jews living in that part of the world at that time, sheep were very important in their lives. Sheep provided food, clothing, and were part of their religious observances. Every family had a few sheep. Most of them did not have very many.

Every day the sheep had to be taken out to find sufficient grazing Whoever was assigned to take the sheep out that day would leave the village in the predawn hours, chanting to the sheep, and the other sheep would follow them. The assigned shepherd would control the sheep all day with that method. In the evening when they returned, whoever had been leading the sheep all day would now enter the village quietly. Along the way, various family members would step out and began their chant. Ears would come up, sheep would peal out of the flock and go into their own folds. The sheep were controlled by voice.

The people standing there that day, did not understand Jesus to say what you understood him to say. They did not hear "Sheep are good and goats are bad." What those people, all of who had both sheep and goats, heard was that he would divide the obedient from the disobedient. I really liked that. It was brand new light on my understanding.

Jesus referred to those who wanted to be known as being his in three terms. These terms were used frequently and interchangeably: followers, disciples, and sheep.

Notice in the passage from Matthew 25, what Jesus said:

When the Son of Man comes in his glory, and all the angels with him, he will sit on his glorious throne. All the nations will be gathered before him, and he will separate the people one from another as a shepherd separates the sheep from the goats. He will put the sheep on his right and the goats on his left.

Jesus is the Son of Man. He will be doing the dividing on that day. What will be the basis of that division?

"Then the King will say to those on his right, 'Come, you who are blessed by my Father; take your inheritance, the kingdom prepared for you since the creation of the world. For I was hungry and you gave me something to eat, I was thirsty and you gave me something to drink, I was a stranger and you invited me in, I needed clothes and you clothed me, I was sick and you looked after me, I was in prison and you came to visit me.'

Notice that they will respond with total astonishment.

"Then the righteous will answer him, 'Lord, when did we see you hungry and feed you, or thirsty and give you something to drink? When did we see you a stranger and invite you in, or needing clothes and clothe you? When did we see you sick or in prison and go to visit you?'"

"Then he will say to those on his left, 'Depart from me, you who are cursed, into the eternal fire prepared for the devil and his angels. For I was hungry and you gave me nothing to eat, I was thirsty and you gave me nothing to drink, I was a stranger and you did not invite me in, I needed clothes and you did not clothe me, I was sick and in prison and you did not look after me.'"

Once again, notice the response of this group.

"They also will answer, 'Lord, when did we see you hungry or thirsty or a stranger or needing clothes or sick or in prison, and did not help you?'

His answer?

"He will reply, 'Truly I tell you, whatever you did not do for one of the least of these, you did not do for me.'

"Then they will go away to eternal punishment, but the righteous to eternal life."

The main point here is that they never recognized their 'Day of Visitation' from on high. It was as they did not serve *others* they did not serve *Him*. The most important matter for any Christian in this arena is to continually answer the question: What am I doing with what God gave me to use in the service of those around me? When a Christian is really intent on being everything they can be for their Lord, especially in relation to the passages we have just finished, I would suggest a concentrated study of the following:

Meditate on this question: How much do you really trust God? Let us proceed with the following verse as background: But seek first his kingdom and his righteousness, and all these things will be given to you as well (Matthew 6:33 NIV).

Let us seek His righteousness for a while. If we would be used by God in and for service to others, consider these passages:

Ask and it will be given to you; seek and you will find; knock and the door will be opened to you. For everyone who asks receives; the one who seeks finds; and to the one who knocks, the door will be opened."

> "Which of you, if your son asks for bread, will give him a stone? Or if he asks for a fish, will give him a snake? If you, then, though you are evil, know how to give good gifts to your children, how much more will your Father in heaven give good gifts to those who ask him!" (Matthew 7:7-11 NIV)

Notice the absence of such qualifying words as maybe, sometimes, possibly, might, could be, if.... No! Jesus used the phrases: "Ask and it will be given to you; seek and you will find; knock and the door will be opened to you." Then He further emphasizes these phrases with the words "For everyone who asks receives; the one who seeks finds; and to the one who knocks, the door will be opened." Then since we might, in our human frailty, miss what He is talking about, He asks, "Which of you, if your son asks for bread, will give him a stone? Or if he asks for a fish, will give him a snake?" Jesus points out that in our human frailty, we would give our children what they needed, not ignore and hurt them. Then He adds this: "If you, then, though you are evil, know how to give good gifts to your children, how much more will your Father in heaven give good gifts to those who ask him!"

Let us add two more verses to these to point out the basis of our need to examine where we are in allowing ourselves to be used of God.

> Again, truly I tell you that if two of you on earth agree about anything they ask for, it will be done for them by my Father in heaven. Matthew 18:19 (NIV)

> If you believe, you will receive whatever you ask for in prayer. (Matthew 21:22 NIV)

And we need to remember another verse: James 4:2b (NIV): "You do not have because you do not ask God."

The Nature of God

The words of an old hymn come to mind at this point:
When we walk with the Lord, in the light of His Word, what a glory He sheds on our way, while we do his goodwill, He abides with us still, and with all who trust and obey!
Trust and obey, for there's no other way, to be happy in Jesus, but to trust and obey.

The question is, how much do you trust God?

I believe it is absolutely necessary for us to be living out the first marching order on love before trying to carry out the second marching order which is to share the gospel. That marching order we find at the conclusion of Matthew's Gospel:

> Then Jesus came to them and said, "All authority in heaven and on earth has been given to me. Therefore go and make disciples of all nations, baptizing them in the name of the Father and of the Son and of the Holy Spirit, and teaching them to obey everything I have commanded you. And surely I am with you always, to the very end of the age." (Matthew 28:18-20 NIV)

It was the conviction of John Wesley that everyone could and should experience God. It was also his conviction that if this confrontation and experience of God did not propel one into ministry, then it did not take! The living out of the first marching order, which I stated was necessary prior to living out the second marching order, is in fact only completed if one does carry it over into the living out of the second marching order.

So this God, the creator, the author and sustainer of life, desires to have a relationship with you. That relationship stated as simply as possible is this: God says, "I will be your God. You be my people." When we get that straight, and when we experience God, we will be a New Creation!

The Greater Reality

It begins with our experiencing Him as the disciples did. They experienced Him in life after they had witnessed his death. They knew He was alive. The world could not take that away from them. Because of that one fact, and that fact alone, they became a new creation.

> While they were still talking about this, Jesus himself stood among them and said to them, "Peace be with you."
>
> They were startled and frightened, thinking they saw a ghost.
> He said to them, "Why are you troubled, and why do doubts rise in your minds? Look at my hands and my feet. It is I myself! Touch me and see; a ghost does not have flesh and bones, as you see I have."
> When he had said this, he showed them his hands and feet. And while they still did not believe it because of joy and amazement, he asked them, "Do you have anything here to eat?"
> They gave him a piece of broiled fish, and he took it and ate it in their presence.
> He said to them, "This is what I told you while I was still with you: Everything must be fulfilled that is written about me in the Law of Moses, the Prophets and the Psalms."
> Then he opened their minds so they could understand the Scriptures. He told them, "This is what is written: The Messiah will suffer and rise from the dead on the third day, and repentance for the forgiveness of sins will be preached in his name to all nations, beginning at Jerusalem. You are witnesses of these things. (Luke 24:36-48 NIV)

Session twenty-four of the Discipleship Bible Study begins with a paragraph entitled, "Our Human Condition": "We believe in God, but we have so little power. We want to witness, to heal, to convert, to serve, to change society; but we are ordinary people. We lack spiritual vitality." Many of us feel like that. There is a solution to this situation. Every year in the spring, we celebrate the wonderful season of Easter. We celebrate Maundy Thursday, Good Friday, and Easter.

The earthly life of Jesus Christ culminated with the trip to Jerusalem, the celebration of that last meal with His disciples in His earthly form, His arrest, the crucifixion on the cross, the burial of His dead body, and then Resurrection. On the cross, He died a horrible death. By that death, He joined humanity it its suffering. And, He arose from the dead proving the promise of eternal life.

Along the way, some things happened that gave us pause for reflection. Jesus repeatedly told them that he was going to Jerusalem to die. On several occasions he warned them that they were going to be tested and that they would fail. Listen to His last warning:

Then Jesus told them, "This very night you will all fall away on account of me, for it is written: "'I will strike the shepherd, and the sheep of the flock will be scattered (Matthew 26:31 NIV). The disciples never received and understood what He was saying before it took place. Listen to their affirmation lead by Peter:

> Peter replied, "Even if all fall away on account of you, I never will."

> "Truly I tell you," Jesus answered, "this very night, before the rooster crows, you will disown me three times."

> But Peter declared, "Even if I have to die with you, I will never disown you." And all the other disciples said the same. (Matthew 26:33-35 NIV)

The Greater Reality

Read that last verse again. And all the other disciples said the same. Every man in that room meant it when he said it. At that moment every disciple felt that he was ready to stand by Jesus and be faithful to Him. I repeat, every disciple meant what he said. They all really felt that they were able to stand. But now, listen to the way it all turned out that night in the Garden of Gethsemane.

We will divide this passage of Scripture into several passages for there are several different things going on here that have to be addressed.

> Then Jesus went with his disciples to a place called Gethsemane, and he said to them, "Sit here while I go over there and pray." He took Peter and the two sons of Zebedee along with him, and he began to be sorrowful and troubled. Then he said to them, "My soul is overwhelmed with sorrow to the point of death. Stay here and keep watch with me."

> Going a little farther, he fell with his face to the ground and prayed, "My Father, if it is possible, may this cup be taken from me. Yet not as I will, but as you will."

> Then he returned to his disciples and found them sleeping. "Couldn't you men keep watch with me for one hour?" he asked Peter. "Watch and pray so that you will not fall into temptation. The spirit is willing, but the flesh is weak."

> He went away a second time and prayed, "My Father, if it is not possible for this cup to be taken away unless I drink it, may your will be done."

When he came back, he again found them sleeping, because their eyes were heavy. So he left them and went away once more and prayed the third time, saying the same thing.

Then he returned to the disciples and said to them, "Are you still sleeping and resting? Look, the hour has come, and the Son of Man is delivered into the hands of sinners. Rise! Let us go! Here comes my betrayer!" (Matthew 26:36-46 NIV)

Here is a thought well worth focusing on for a few minutes. Jesus prepared Himself for the coming ordeal by spending this time with the Father. On His knees pouring out his heart to the Father, Jesus won the upcoming battle of the cross, the night before it took place.

The disciples were tired, and they fell asleep. To put it another way, they took care of their bodies. Their bodies were not going to do them any good that night or the next day. They failed to make preparation when that preparation would do them some good. The coming battle was not going to be a physical battle but a spiritual one. They missed their opportunity to get ready. That is one reason they failed later.

Now the conclusion of the garden scene:

While he was still speaking, Judas, one of the Twelve, arrived. With him was a large crowd armed with swords and clubs, sent from the chief priests and the elders of the people. Now the betrayer had arranged a signal with them: "The one I kiss is the man; arrest him."

Going at once to Jesus, Judas said, "Greetings, Rabbi!" and kissed him.

Jesus replied, "Do what you came for, friend."

Then the men stepped forward, seized Jesus and arrested him. With that, one of Jesus' companions reached for his sword, drew it out and struck the servant of the high priest, cutting off his ear.

"Put your sword back in its place," Jesus said to him, "for all who draw the sword will die by the sword. Do you think I cannot call on my Father, and he will at once put at my disposal more than twelve legions of angels? But how then would the Scriptures be fulfilled that say it must happen in this way?"

In that hour Jesus said to the crowd, "Am I leading a rebellion, that you have come out with swords and clubs to capture me? Every day I sat in the temple courts teaching, and you did not arrest me. But this has all taken place that the writings of the prophets might be fulfilled." Then all the disciples deserted him and fled. (Matthew 26:47-56 NIV)

After following Him, and after living with Him, these eleven men, who had vowed they would not fail Him, failed right down to the last man. It says, "all the disciples deserted him and fled." Our Lord died alone on that hilltop those two thousand years ago. Not one of those who said they would stand by Him stood by Him. Not one! As I said earlier, part of the reason they failed was they did not prepare that night in the Garden of Gethsemane. Jesus prepared. They did not. There is another reason just as important, if not more important than that.

Those cowards, those eleven cowards, needed to be transformed. And, they were.

> While they were still talking about this, Jesus himself stood among them and said to them, "Peace be with you."
> They were startled and frightened, thinking they saw a ghost.
> He said to them, "Why are you troubled, and why do doubts rise in your minds? Look at my hands and my feet. It is I myself! Touch me and see; a ghost does not have flesh and bones, as you see I have."
> When he had said this, he showed them his hands and feet. And while they still did not believe it because of joy and amazement, he asked them, "Do you have anything here to eat?"
> They gave him a piece of broiled fish, and he took it and ate it in their presence. (Luke 24:36-43 NIV)

The point I want to make here is that these men experienced Jesus in life after death. They had seen Him die. Now they experienced Him in life again after death. This was not an apparition. Jesus Himself was standing there in their midst. God happened to them. Later, in addition, the Holy Spirit would be given to them on the Day of Pentecost. God happened to them. The Holy Spirit was given to them, and they were transformed.

There is another passage which I find very interesting.

> Afterward Jesus appeared again to his disciples, by the Sea of Galilee. It happened this way: Simon Peter, Thomas (also known as Didymus), Nathanael from Cana in Galilee, the sons of Zebedee, and two other disciples were together. "I'm going out to fish," Simon Peter told them, and they said, "We'll go with you." So they went out and got into the boat, but that night they caught nothing.

Early in the morning, Jesus stood on the shore, but the disciples did not realize that it was Jesus.
He called out to them, "Friends, haven't you any fish?" "No," they answered.
He said, "Throw your net on the right side of the boat and you will find some." When they did, they were unable to haul the net in because of the large number of fish.
Then the disciple whom Jesus loved said to Peter, "It is the Lord!" As soon as Simon Peter heard him say, "It is the Lord," he wrapped his outer garment around him (for he had taken it off) and jumped into the water. The other disciples followed in the boat, towing the net full of fish, for they were not far from shore, about a hundred yards. When they landed, they saw a fire of burning coals there with fish on it, and some bread.
Jesus said to them, "Bring some of the fish you have just caught." So Simon Peter climbed back into the boat and dragged the net ashore. It was full of large fish, 153, but even with so many the net was not torn. Jesus said to them, "Come and have breakfast."
None of the disciples dared ask him, "Who are you?" They knew it was the Lord. Jesus came, took the bread and gave it to them, and did the same with the fish. This was now the third time Jesus appeared to his disciples after he was raised from the dead. (John 21:1-14 NIV)

Please notice something here of very great importance. Our Lord is in the middle of the plan of salvation for all humankind. In the midst of that terribly important plan, He had time to take care of the needs of those disciples. He fed them breakfast. Wow!

Many years ago, our church hosted a choir from California called "The Continentals." They sang a very special song

The Nature of God

which I heard for the first time, "He's Alive." The song centers on the thoughts that first Easter morning of the Apostle Peter.

The disciples gathered in an upper room in total desolation. Jesus had died. He was buried. Their world had been turned upside down. Because even though He had told them it was coming, and they had heard, they had not understood any of it until later. In the song, it is pointed out that Peter was desolate. I think the song has it right. Peter was probably the most desolate of all. He knew his failure more than anyone else.

There is a passage in the song that takes place just after Mary said, "He is alive!"

It goes like this: "Even if He is alive, it wouldn't be the same, because when it came to choices, I denied I knew His name."

I believe that those words are really accurate. I also think that Jesus knew they were suffering over their great failure. At that point, Jesus appears to the disciples. They see Him in life after death. They had to have that. Once again, beloved, they experienced Jesus that first Easter morning.

Listen, a few days later as Jesus takes care of one more piece of business. He believes is so very necessary before the ascension into heaven.

> When they had finished eating, Jesus said to Simon Peter, "Simon son of John, do you love me more than these?"
> "Yes, Lord," he said, "you know that I love you."
> Jesus said, "Feed my lambs."
> Again Jesus said, "Simon son of John, do you love me?"
> He answered, "Yes, Lord, you know that I love you."
> Jesus said, "Take care of my sheep."
> The third time he said to him, "Simon son of John, do you love me?"

> Peter was hurt because Jesus asked him the third time, "Do you love me?" He said, "Lord, you know all things; you know that I love you."
> Jesus said, "Feed my sheep. Very truly I tell you, when you were younger you dressed yourself and went where you wanted; but when you are old you will stretch out your hands, and someone else will dress you and lead you where you do not want to go." Jesus said this to indicate the kind of death by which Peter would glorify God. Then he said to him, "Follow me!" John 21:15-19 (NIV)

You all know what is taking place here. Jesus is giving Peter the opportunity to affirm three times again his love for Jesus. Pete had denied Him three times. Jesus is giving him the opportunity to affirm Him three times.

Before His crucifixion, Peter had said, "Even if all fall away on account of you, I never will."

Jesus had responded, "Truly I tell you," Jesus answered, "this very night, before the rooster crows, you will disown me three times."

This time after Peter declares his love for Jesus, Jesus makes quite a different response. Listen to it:

> Jesus said, "Feed my sheep. Very truly I tell you, when you were younger you dressed yourself and went where you wanted; but when you are old you will stretch out your hands, and someone else will dress you and lead you where you do not want to go." Jesus said this to indicate the kind of death by which Peter would glorify God. Then he said to him, "Follow me!"

The first time, Jesus had said, "You will fail me," but this time he says, "Yes, you will stand true, and you will die keeping your word about loving me. How did this take place? Church tradition tells us that these men never failed again. To the last man they died proclaiming the gospel of Jesus Christ. Folks, they were transformed. They were new men.

The key phrase is: They were transformed. God happened to them. Maybe one reason the church is dying in so many places today is, you just cannot sell something you do not have. Many people sitting in church pews today have a form of Godliness, but they do not have God. We need God to happen to us.

The disciples experienced God. Those eleven men turned their world upside down.

If you do not like the way things are today, listen to this promise from God.

"If my people, who are called by my name, will humble themselves and pray and seek my face and turn from their wicked ways, then I will hear from heaven, and I will forgive their sin and will heal their land" (2 Chronicles 7:14 NIV).

This is the key. Every person needs to let God happen to them.

LIVING A LIFE OF GRATITUDE

When God happens to a person and they become that new creation, their life will become a life of gratitude. One's attitude makes all the difference in the world as to how they face trials and tribulations. It has often been stated, that it is not the circumstances that one faces in life that determine failure or victory in life, it is how one deals with those circumstances. Listen to the Apostle Paul; he had discovered that truth:

> I have learned to be content whatever the circumstances. I know what it is to be in need, and I know what it is to have plenty. I have learned the secret of being content in any and every situation, whether well fed or hungry, whether living in plenty or in want. I can do all this through him who gives me strength. (Philippians 4: 11b-13 NIV)

Paul was stoned, beaten with rods, left for dead, spent much time in prison, and knew his time on earth was going to be very limited. He knew he would die young. Yet he said, "I have learned the secret of being content in any and every situation, whether well fed or hungry, whether living in plenty or in want. I can do all this through him who gives me strength."

The question is, do you have the same confidence, serenity, and attitude towards life and all life's circumstances that come your way? It was the discovery of that secret that allowed him to write verses eight and nine of that same chapter:

> Finally, brothers and sisters, whatever is true, whatever is noble, whatever is right, whatever is pure, whatever is lovely, whatever is admirable—if anything is excellent or praiseworthy—think about such things. Whatever you have learned or received or heard from me, or seen in me—put it into practice. And the God of peace will be with you.

The discovery of those truths was the source of his admonishment to the church at Corinth: "So it is with you. Since you are eager for gifts of the Spirit, try to excel in those that build up the church" (1 Corinthians 14:12 NIV).

I was thinking about this subject one day while at Disney World. I observed a man wearing a shirt which had on the front of it, the word *Attitude* in black letters preceded by the two letters *GR* in a bright color. Those two letters extended the base word *Attitude* into a larger word *Gratitude*. I felt God said to me, "That is what is missing in much of the church today." Much of the church does not understand that it is our gratitude or lack of it that determines which direction we look from where we stand. Gratitude determines our attitude. Let's explain that.

Let's say we were placed in living quarters on a very long street where the houses begin on one end of the economic scale with cardboard shacks and they progress up the economic scale to large, columned mansions at the other end of the street, These are on a continual and progressive scale from the one end of the spectrum to the other. We have been placed exactly in the middle in this series of houses. In other words, there are as many people who live in lesser living quarters below our house as there are people who live in more extravagant living quarters above our house. This is the question: Which way will we tend to look? Will we look at those who are less fortunate and count our blessings, or, in our usual human frailty, will we tend to look at those who have more and question why we don't have all their status and position, or why don't we have their larger house? We have that kind of problem in the arena of material things.

We also have the same problem in relationships. We can really hold grudges pretty well, can we not? Someone once said, "Being recipients of grace such as we are, how easy it ought to be for us to forgive others their real and imaginary offenses and transgressions committed against us." Recipients of Grace: Grace ... let's further examine that word.

Dr. James Harnish wrote a book with the help of several leaders from his church entitled *A Disciple's Path*. In that book, grace is discussed several times. I love the following paragraph.

> Grace is the undeserved, unearned, unrepayable gift of the God who loves us enough to meet us where we are, but loves us too much to leave us there. Grace is the love of God at work within us to transform each of our lives into a unique expression of the love of God revealed in Jesus Christ, so that we become participants in God's transformation of the world.

> When you and I were the farthest from the cross, when it was absolutely the most impossible for us to come home, when we were absolutely at our worst, that was when the cross of Christ was for us. "Grace is the undeserved, unearned, unrepayable gift of the God who loves us enough to meet us where we are, but loves us too much to leave us there.

Salvation is the gift of God. You have received as the book said, an undeserved, unearned, unrepayable gift from God.

In the Hebrews 12:1-2 we read:

> Therefore, since we are surrounded by such a great cloud of witnesses, let us throw off everything that hinders and the sin that so easily entangles. And let us run with perseverance the race marked out for us, fixing our eyes on Jesus, the pioneer and perfecter of faith. For the joy set before him he endured the cross, scorning its shame, and sat down at the right hand of the throne of God. (Hebrews 12:1-2 NIV)

Look at those words: "For the joy set before him he endured the cross... Dwell on those words... For the joy set before him he endured the cross." Joy? That Friday, Jesus had already gone through a night of physical torture and pain. Added to the physical torture and pain was the loneliness. All those who had promised they would stand beside him had melted into the darkness the night before.

On the cross, Jesus' life was literally ripped from his body. Hanging on those sensitive points of hands and feet, he slowly suffocated. His breathing shut off from the position he was in. All of that did not bring a cry from Him. But when the Father withdrew as He had to do, the agony of being alone without anyone, including the Father, finally brought forth a cry.

But the Scriptures say, "For the joy set before him he endured the cross, scorning its shame, and sat down at the right hand of the throne of God."

Paul said, "And let us run with perseverance the race marked out for us, fixing our eyes on Jesus, the pioneer and perfecter of faith." Some will say, "If you knew what I am going through, you would not challenge me." But there are those who live in victory and with an attitude of gratitude even though they are caught in circumstances they did not ask for.

The Greater Reality

I have seen them: I have witnessed them: People who live in an attitude of gratitude in spite of their circumstances. Is their frustration and despair real? Of course! In spite of that, they live in victory.

Our grandson and his wife lost a baby. This little one would have been their third child. But something went wrong and the little one did not make it through the nine months. In the announcement to family and friends, his wife shared their hurt and pain. Their pain was very real. But she did not dwell on that. What she focused on was their gratitude and joy. She shared that it had been a source of joy, the giving of life to the little one inside her. She shared how this loss had increased their deep gratitude and joy for the two children they have.

Folks, to put it simply, these two people living in the reality of pain also possessed an attitude of gratitude and allowed it to carry them through their hurt and pain. Pain and reality were very real for them, but there was another reality greater than their pain which carried them above and beyond the present reality.

Most of you have seen the movie by Mel Gibson, *The Passion of Christ*. When you watched it, did you remember that He suffered all of that for you? It was for the whole world. But what should have been hitting you during the showing of those horrible scenes was, *it was for you*. The cross was for you. Jesus Christ went to the Cross for your salvation, now and for eternity.

Everything in the Bible supports that message. Everything in the Bible is about covenant. God wants to have a relationship with you. God wants to live in, with, and through you. God wants to live through you to the extent that the rest of the world will get a vision of Him through you as they interact with you. When you get that straight, it will change your life. Your view will be a view of gratitude. You will live in an attitude of gratitude. And beloved, those who witness your life will not be able to miss that one fact. They will know you are a grateful person.

Many years ago, in a small rural Russian village there lived an old angry recluse. He kept to himself and had almost no interaction with the others in his village. He kept a large, vicious dog. A young couple got married and moved into a house next door to the old man, and several months later, she gave birth to a baby boy. They worried about the dog next door. They watched their son with great care. For a few years, everything was okay. Then one day, the little boy wandered outside his yard and into the neighbor's yard. The vicious dog attacked the little boy and killed him. Everyone believed that the old man had witnessed this and had done nothing to stop the attack. The village was in an uproar. They called a meeting of the townsfolk and everyone wanted to drive the old man from their village. But the parents of the little boy would not allow them to do so.

That winter and spring were very harsh. Everyone's first planting was frozen out. They all had to replant. The old man did not have enough money to buy seed and replant his ground. The people were happy about that. They said, "Good. Now maybe he will leave." But in the middle of one night, someone replanted the old man's ground. An investigation revealed that the father of the little boy was the one who had replanted the old man's ground.

He was asked, "Why did you replant his ground after he allowed his dog to kill your son? How could you do that?"

He replied, "I did it so God could live in my heart again."

In a United Methodist church in Florida, there is a ministry reaching out to migrant workers and their families.

These are people who live below the poverty line. We pick up little children who live in mobile homes, some of which are missing doors and windows. Sometimes they do not get enough to eat, especially on weekends. The church's ministry feeds them both physically and spiritually on Saturdays

The Greater Reality

called "Cereal Saturday." On Sundays they are picked up and brought to the home church for Sunday school and worship. It was my great privilege to drive a load of children back across town one Sunday several months ago. They were singing songs from their Sunday school that morning. Caucasians sing with the brakes on. These children sing with the brakes off. I was just listening and enjoying it. As they finished a song, the little girl sitting up beside me gave a great sigh, looked out the window and said, "I just love church."

I felt compelled to respond. I asked, "Do you like school?'

She said, "I guess I love just about everything."

I thought, "Some of us could learn a lot from her."

A few weeks later, she was going out the church door after being baptized and a woman said joyously to her, "We are very glad to have you here."

She looked at the lady, shrugged her shoulders and responded very matter of fact, "It's my church."

Gratitude!\

The cross was for you. What have you done with it? What do you want to do with it?

This little girl had so little to be grateful for. Yet, she lived with true joy in her heart for everyone and everything. Her circumstances did not control her outlook on life. We could learn so much from her.

There is another aspect of our understanding of God that is very important if we are going to be free to live in honest gratitude towards God and all that God gives us. We shared earlier that it is in God's nature that He desires to have a relationship with us. It is for that purpose that we were created in the first place. Here is a thought that I believe is very important for every person on earth to understand. We believe that God is in charge of this universe. Every person who believes in God really does believe that. But sometimes we do not think that fact through and end up with a misunderstanding of God which prevents us from leaning on and trusting in God totally. You see this each time something happens which we do fully understand or cannot explain.

People will say, "I wonder what they did that God did that to them." Alternatively, if they do not want to go that far, they may say, "I wonder what they did that God let that happen to them?" Either way, God gets blamed. The truth is, God does not cause the bad things that happen to people. I believe that God gets blamed for a lot of things that He does not do. Stop and consider what I am saying for just a moment. If God is in direct control of everything, then you and I are just puppets on a string. There cannot be a day of judgment for us. Why is that true? It would be true because we did not do anything. God did it. So on the Day of Judgment, God would be on trial, not us.

The truth is that God's Will is divided into two parts. There is God's directed will, and there is God's permissive will. Sometimes we come under God's directed will if we surrender to Him and try our best to follow Him and be obedient to Him. We should do that because the God of the universe who created that universe desires to have a relationship with us now and throughout eternity. But even those who try desperately to come under His directed will do not do it perfectly.

Listen to the testimony of the apostle Paul, the greatest missionary heart and the greatest theological mind that ever lived:

> We know that the law is spiritual; but I am unspiritual, sold as a slave to sin. I do not understand what I do. For what I want to do I do not do, but what I hate I do. And if I do what I do not want to do, I agree that the law is good. As it is, it is no longer I myself who do it, but it is sin living in me. I know that nothing good lives in me, that is, in my sinful nature. For I have the desire to do what is good, but I cannot carry it out. For what I do is not the good I want to do; no, the evil I

do not want to do—this I keep on doing. Now if I do what I do not want to do, it is no longer I who do it, but it is sin living in me that does it.

So I find this law at work: When I want to do good, evil is right there with me. For in my inner being I delight in God's law; but I see another law at work in the members of my body, waging war against the law of my mind and making me a prisoner of the law of sin at work within my members. What a wretched man I am! Who will rescue me from this body of death? Thanks be to God—through Jesus Christ our Lord! (Romans 7:14-25 NIV)

I believe it is very important to get that truth straight. God does not cause our pain. God put us here on earth. Our lives are intermingled with the lives of many others. None of us are perfect. And because we live most of the time under God's permissive will, we do experience sometimes in our lives pain, even great pain.

God forgives sin and then He forgets it. This is His Word to us. Isaiah 43:25 (NIV) says, "I, even I, am he who blots out your transgressions, for my own sake, and remembers your sins no more."

When we go to God with a repentant heart and ask His forgiveness for anything and are really repentant, searching for our relationship with Him to be restored again, God hears our prayers and forgives and even forgets our sins. There are still consequences of wrong actions that we have to live with. Wrong actions always result in wrong consequences. Even though actions can be forgiven, we will oftentimes have to live with the consequences. That truth covers all of life. In the midst of this, what is now of greatest importance? I want people to know that God did not cause their hurt, but God is there and God will carry them through.

No one will be able to stand up against you all the days of your life. As I was with Moses, so I will be with you; I will never leave you nor forsake you. (Joshua 1:5 NIV)

I will not leave you as orphans; I will come to you. (John 14:18-19 NIV)

And I will ask the Father, and he will give you another Counselor to be with you forever—the Spirit of truth. (John 14:16-17a NIV)

Now two verses that bring all of this together:

The Lord appeared to us in the past, saying: "I have loved you with an everlasting love; I have drawn you with loving-kindness. (Jeremiah 31:3 NIV)

And we know that in all things God works for the good of those who love him, who have been called according to his purpose. (Romans 8:28 NIV)

That last verse simply says that out of even the bad things that happen to us, God can bring good for us, if we will allow Him to. But understand the following truth: God said of the children of Israel that they were His chosen people. "I who set the heavens in place, who laid the foundations of the earth, and who say to Zion, 'You are my people'" (Isaiah 51:16b NIV) But God was never obligated to reward their disobedience. When they made the decision from time to time to be disobedient, they were free to do so. When they were disobedient to His will, they also moved out from under the umbrella of protection that was theirs when they walked in obedience with God. When they returned to Him, He forgave their sins and began blessing their walk of obedience and harmony was restored.

POSTLUDE

In this book I have shared the stories of several people whose lives I have witnessed. They have been caught in a reality that we could not miss, but who obviously had their eyes focused on another reality that we could not see that was carrying them over the reality which we could see. To put it another way, they have been living in victory.

There are many other stories of people while not living quite the dramatic lives as these who also lived in victory. I like to say, they live in an attitude of gratitude. That phrase first came to me many years ago in the story of Thelma Thompson.

Thelma had arrived to live in a village at the edge of the desert to be near her husband who was stationed during World War II at an army training camp in the vicinity. The Mojave desert in California is a place of dust, fierce winds, and unbearable heat. The Mexican Indians who inhabit this area lead a life apart and speak no English. Alone while her husband was away on maneuvers, she felt isolated. It was impossible to make contact with the local people, thanks to the language barrier. The environment was also hostile. It was very dry, which she was not used to. The wind blew constantly. There was dust on everything: the floors, the furniture, on her clothes, and on the food. Finally she decided that she had had enough. She wrote to tell her parents that she wanted to come home. She sent a telegram, asking her father to wire her money. She would wait at the telegraph office to receive it.

His answer both surprised and angered her. The reply she received from her father considered of just two lines: "Two men looked out from prison bars, one saw mud, the other saw stars. Love Dad,"

She read that message over and over again. When she finally worked through it, she felt ashamed of her decision to leave. Thelma made up her mind to see "the stars" in her situation, rather than the "mud." It was a decision that was to alter her entire life. Making friends with the natives, she learned their languages and culture and began to see desert life in a new light. She watched the magnificent desert sunsets and studied the cacti, the yuccas, and the Joshua trees in all their fascinating variety. She even hunted for seashells that had been left there millions of years ago when the sands of the desert had been an ocean floor. Gradually the region began to exercise such a fascination over her mind that both she and her husband decided to stay on after he had retired from military service.

Thelma became recognized nationally as an authority on the Navajo Turquoise jewelry, and she later wrote a novel, *Bright Ramparts*, which expressed all the excitement she had felt over her new experiences and discoveries. Her book proved very popular and ran to several editions.

A wretched experience had been transformed into an exciting adventure. But how exactly had this transformation taken place? Neither the desert, nor the natives, nor any other element in the situation had changed. Whenever we analyze suffering, we find that there are two main features to it. One is the thing which causes the suffering and the other is our own reaction to it. We should take courage from Thelma Thomson's example, and so control our reaction that suffering is finally eliminated. Whatever change had taken place was inside the mind heart of Thelma Thompson. Her own change of attitude had given her a new life.

We all have the choice of either living in an attitude of gratitude, or having some other attitude. My journey is about ended. I am in, at least, the "fall" season of my life, if not the "winter." I can honestly say that the only time I have experienced defeat in my journey was brought on when I moved away from living in an attitude of gratitude. Every person is human, including pastors. It is easy for any human being to focus in the mirror and go on a pity party. It can be brought on by extreme fatigue, perceived disrespect, the pressure of others, or too much of the world's materials.

When Jesus talked about the "four soils," pastors are almost never the first where the seed lay on top of the ground and never took root. But every person in any Christian vocation can very easily become the second soil, rocky ground where there was no depth.

In the very first "Pastors School" I attended, one of our leaders said, "Be very careful when you get back to your parishes that you do not let the good things crowd out the best." What he meant by that statement was that we can fill our lives with all kinds of good things to the extent that we do not take necessary time out to anchor ourselves deep in Scripture and prayer. When we neglect spiritual disciplines, we open ourselves to danger and failure in that we try to do God's work in man's strength. We become that shallow soil.

Every person in any Christian vocation can very easily become the third soil, weedy ground where the spiritual life is crowded out by the cares of this world. We become the fourth soil that brings in its increase when we nourish ourselves in spiritual disciples. We spend that necessary time in God's Word and with God in prayer.

One of my very favorite movies is *Fiddler on the Roof*. It began as a Broadway musical in 1964, and the movie version came out in 1971. I saw the movie first in 1972. In that movie,

Postlude

Tevye talks to God just like you would talk to a friend, and, he talks everything over with his Friend. On one occasion, Tevye is walking along pulling his cart with the horse tied on and limping behind the cart. Tevye looks up and says, "I know you have to pick on me, but did you have to pick on my horse?"

The first time I heard that, I thought, "Watch out, lightning is going to hit you."

But then when I thought about it, I came to a very different conclusion. I wished for every person in my congregation to have that very same understanding. I wish every person sitting in the pew thought of God as being right there just off his or her shoulder. I wish they talked always as if God was listening, because in reality, God is right there. That is the kind of relationship that God wants to have with us. It is the intimacy God desires to have with us. That is what the covenant relationship is.

Tevye had that kind of relationship because of time spent time with God, both in prayer, which was conversational, and time listening to Scriptures being discussed.

Let us return to a thought shared earlier about the intimacy that God wants to have with us. The following Scripture defines God's desire for us.

> I tell you the truth, the man who does not enter the sheep pen by the gate, but climbs in by some other way, is a thief and a robber. The man who enters by the gate is the shepherd of his sheep. The watchman opens the gate for him, and the sheep listen to his voice. He calls his own sheep by name and leads them out. When he has brought out all his own, he goes on ahead of them, and his sheep follow him because they know his voice. But they will never follow a stranger; in fact, they will run away from him because they do not recognize a stranger's voice.

Jesus used this figure of speech, but they did not understand what He was telling them.

Therefore Jesus said again, "I tell you the truth, I am the gate for the sheep. All who ever came before me were thieves and robbers, but the sheep did not listen to them. I am the gate; whoever enters through me will be saved. He will come in and go out, and find pasture. The thief comes only to steal and kill and destroy; I have come that they might have life, and have it to the full." (John 10:1-10 NASB)

Again, hold that passage in mind while we return to the passage that gives additional light to our topic:

When the Son of Man comes in his glory, and all the angels with him, he will sit on his throne in heavenly glory. All the nations will be gathered before him, and he will separate the people one from another as a shepherd separates the sheep from the goats. He will put the sheep on his right and the goats on his left. (Matthew 25:31-33 NIV)

I shared with you how it had been my practice, just after I read that part where Jesus said he would divide those before him as a shepherd divides the sheep from the goats, to make the following statement. "When I get to heaven, I want to ask why sheep were arbitrarily good while goats were arbitrarily bad." Recall the conversation with that visiting rancher when he asked if he could comment on the sermon? He asked if I had ever worked with sheep or goats.

He shared about sheep being followers: "Sheep will follow you wherever you lead them. Sheep are obedient. You have to pen them up to keep them from following you. Goats, you cannot even drive them. They will fight you every step of the way."

He gave me that new light that the people standing there that day did not hear 'Sheep are good and goats are bad.' What those people, all of who had both sheep and goats, heard was he would divide the 'obedient from the disobedient.'"

We shared how Jesus used three words frequently and interchangeably: followers, disciples, and sheep.

Jesus said:

> The man who enters by the gate is the shepherd of his sheep. The watchman opens the gate for him, and the sheep listen to his voice. He calls his own sheep by name and leads them out. When he has brought out all his own, he goes on ahead of them, and his sheep follow him because they know his voice. But they will never follow a stranger; in fact, they will run away from him because they do not recognize a stranger's voice. (John 10:2-5 NIV)

The rancher was correct. Sheep are followers. Today there are people who still control their sheep with the voice.

In John's gospel, Jesus said:

> He calls his own sheep by name and leads them out. When he has brought out all his own, he goes on ahead of them, and his sheep follow him because they know his voice. But they will never follow a stranger; in fact, they will run away from him because they do not recognize a stranger's voice. (John 10:3b-5 NIV)

The reason this worked was that when a lamb was born, it hit the ground hearing the chant of its shepherd and owner. It was fed with the same chant. It was put to bed and awakened with that chant. That chant was literally burned into its brain. One cannot go down to the local sale barn, buy some sheep, and have the voice control thing work. It only worked because of time spent together.

The same thing is true for us today. When Jesus said that his sheep knew his voice, they only knew it because of time spent together. You and I will only recognize His voice if we are deep into His Word, if there is regular time spent in prayer, and if we are fellowshipping with the saints. Saints are those who love Him, and saints are growing in Him. Growth means Bible study, prayer, and conversation with others who also love and desire to follow the shepherd.

John Wesley, the founder of all Wesleyan Theological churches, believed we should all be on a lifelong search for truth. For Wesley, this search should take place within the boundaries of four guidelines. Those guidelines are Scripture first, tradition second, next experience, and finally reason. I challenge you to make sure that Scripture is first and that it always remain the primary.

Today we have such a proliferation of material out there. Many church people read someone's book first. Then they measure Scripture against it. That is the reverse of what God would have you do. Scripture is first and primary. First read God's Word, and then bounce any other book off of it.

Tradition? What did our forefathers in the church say that a given passage says? What do others today say about what that passage says? You may not arrive at the same conclusion they did. But if you only read it, and never allow others to feed in, you will gradually come to the place where you only regurgitate back your own thoughts. Bible study groups as well as the past are important.

Experience? You have lived. You have life experiences. They are a part of your understanding.

Reason? Your faith should make sense.

We also nourish ourselves in spiritual disciplines when we have that fellowship with the saints. A victorious Christian

Postlude

will be sharing in fellowship and growth with God's children in groups that provide Christian nurture.

Finally, one will very naturally live in gratitude when they focus on the gifts of God rather than what the rest of the world might temporarily possess. We will never in this temporary arena come close to giving back to God what God has already given, is giving, and promises for the future.

May the Grace of God continue to be with you!

It will, if you will only allow it.

"I am the good shepherd; and I know My own, and My own know Me, even as the Father knows Me and I know the Father; and I lay down My life for the sheep." (John 10:14-15 NASB)

CPSIA information can be obtained at www.ICGtesting.com
Printed in the USA
LVOW04s2121030914

402307LV00010B/159/P